The Old Berkshire
Village Book

The Old Berkshire Village Book

Compiled by the Berkshire
Federation of Women's Institutes from notes
sent by Institutes in the County

Published jointly by
Countryside Books, Newbury
and the B.F.W.I., Reading

First published in 1972 as Berkshire Village Book
New Edition 1979
Reprinted 1980, 1981

© Berkshire Federation of Women's Institutes 1979

The B.F.W.I. record their grateful thanks to all
Institutes whose members gathered the information
about their villages.
To Kay Abson of East Hendred, for the delightful
line illustrations.
To Joan Colyer, of Priestwood, for the fine picture
map.
To the Village Book Committee . . .
Doris Fardon, Miranda Mayne, Joyce Millward,
Angela Perkins, Eileen Shorland and Brenda Stirling.

Cover Photograph by H. H. Dennis
Cover Design by Mon Mohan
Printed by Maund and Irvine Ltd., Tring, Herts.

Foreword

This new issue of Berkshire Village Book will be welcomed, not only by the dwellers in the county, some of whom compiled it, but by many visitors from afar.

Our Royal County is famous for the diversity of its scenery. Some of its loveliest villages border the Rivers Thames, Kennet, and Lambourn. There are others, equally attractive, set in the folds of the Downs or in the pleasant fields below the Ridgeway. Most of them are described here, mainly by members of the local Women's Institute, whose intimate knowledge of their particular villages adds zest and freshness to their contributions.

As well as brief historical notes, there are local legends, character sketches, fascinating examples of Berkshire dialect, and some flashes of pure poetry when some particularly beautiful spot is described by one who lives with it and clearly loves it.

This little book does not pretend to be a guide book in the sense that a gazeteer is. There are plenty of excellent guides to Berkshire, complete with maps, population figures, market days and the like. This is something more. It is a compilation by Berkshire people about the county in which they take pride and pleasure, and which they want to share with others.

It is a unique record of a wide choice of villages, a rich slice of social history, written with matchless enthusiasm.

It is good to see it in print again.

Miss Read
Shefford Woodlands
February, 1979

ROYAL COUNTY OF BERKSHIRE

Berkshire

The Royal County of Berkshire is tightly woven into the elaborate pattern of English history. Its past and present are the result of the geographical lie of the land . . . London, the timeless capital city, lies close at hand to the east, and Windsor Castle rises up in splendour to proclaim that whatsoever monarch shall reign, Berkshire is a royal domain.

The northern boundary of the county is the winding River Thames, first and greatest highway from east to west. The natural "green roads" of the Ancient Britons cross the county on the high lands . . . the Icknield Way and the Ridgeway have been worn by countless passing feet, by horsemen, armies, invaders, by flocks of sheep and cattle.

The great Roman roads go up and down the hills and valleys and plains, over the fords and bridges, beside the little towns and villages.

Because the roads and tracks and rivers were there, the little settlements grew up beside them. Basically, Berkshire villages follow a familiar pattern, and the pattern is Saxon . . . the little church, the manor, the farms and cottages clustered round, and the strip farming land adjacent to the village. Later additions were the village green, the school, the hall, the all-purpose shop, and the craftsmen. Some settlements have remained remarkably unchanged through the centuries, mainly where the Squire has kept a strict, paternal grip on all development within the manor. Others have grown and diversified, with rich additions in architecture and ways of life . . . it is all there to be read in stone, brick, plaster and thatch.

The monasteries, priories and churches have left their imprints; so have the fortifications and moats and great, staunch houses; the barns and dovecotes and humble little dwellings; the lovely bridges and the useful mills, as well as the relentless signs of the Industrial Revolution.

Many rural settlements have been swallowed up by the growing towns . . . the surprising fact is that so many beautiful and interesting Berkshire villages still survive.

While they are still there to be seen and valued and parts of our county remain green and pleasant, this little book has been gathered together as a record.

We make no claim that this is a work of scholarship, or that there is not a great deal more to be said and written about the villages of Berkshire.

1

We do claim that we who live in the villages have unique advantages in finding out some of the interesting pages of the past. We know what our countryside looks like, and what is there for the visitors to see. Some of our local stories are hallowed by tradition but difficult to prove . . . we have tried to make this clear.

Many people have had a hand in gathering in this information, and it has been a labour of love. The main problem has been the ruthless pruning and discarding of all sorts of fascinating material for which there simply was no room . . . a dozen large books could have been written, but we were committed to one of a specific size.

It will slip comfortably into your car or bookshelf, and introduce the reader and the visitor to the great variety and many delights of this ancient part of England.

Since the first edition of this book was published there has been the great upheaval of local government and boundary changes. The northern 'hump' of Berkshire has become part of Oxfordshire. Sadly the Royal County has lost many beautiful and ancient villages . . . but the villages are still where they were, and the people who live in them, and supplied the information, maintain their interest and pride in their heritage. What's in a name? The Old Berkshire Village Book covers it all.

MIRANDA MAYNE

"Being to take my leave of this Shire, I seriously considered what want there was therein so that I might wish it the supply thereof. But I can discover no natural defect. And I therefore wish the inhabitants a thankful heart to that God who hath given them a County so perfect in profit and pleasure—"

THOMAS FULLER, 1608 - 61.

2

Aldworth is a small village on the edge of the Downs at the top of two steep hills, Apple Pie Hill leading up from Compton, and Streatley Hill leading on down to the Thames. Named in Domesday Book as Elleorde, the "Old Town", a branch of the Ridgeway runs through the parish and there is a section of Grimsdyke (Devil's Ditch) near De la Beche.

The centre of interest in the village is the church, St. Mary's, dating from the 12th century. In the church are the famous 14th-century monuments of the De la Beche family, "the Aldworth giants". There are nine recumbent stone figures, three lying against the north wall, three against the south wall under floriated arches. The remaining three lie on stone slabs in the body of the church. Represented are three generations of one family who lived at Aldworth during the 13th and 14th centuries—the figures are very much damaged. A Captain Symonds in the time of Charles 1st visited the church and made notes and drawings which survive. He says: "In the east end of the south aisle did hang a table fairly written on parchment of all the names of this family of De la Beche; but the Earl of Leicester coming with Queen Elizabeth in progress, took it down to shew it her and it was never brought again". The Queen is said to have ridden from Ewelme to inspect these celebrated tombs.

On the north wall lie the figures of Sir Robert, Sir John and the giant Sir Philip; those of another Sir John and Isabelle his wife lie, side by side, on a large tomb at the entrance to the chancel. Both are damaged and mutilated.

Two more figures of men lie along the south wall, and under the middle arch between them lies the figure of Joan, wife of Sir Nicholas, the most distinguished of his family. He was high in the favour of Edward III, had the charge of the young Black Prince and was later Constable of the Tower. In 1338 he obtained a licence from the King to crenellate his manor house of De la Beche and make it a castle. He died in 1345 and his figure lies in the middle of the church, wearing a helmet and resting his head on a shield.

There is a legend that a tenth stone figure was buried under the outer wall of the church. Symonds says, "The common people call the statue under the outside of the church 'John Everafraid', and say further that he gave his soul to the devil if ever he was buried in either church or churchyard—so he was buried under church wall, under an arch". In the churchyard stand the remains of a great yew tree which was believed to be older than the church.

The castle of the De la Beches stood about half a mile to the south, where the manor house now stands. Encaustic tiles, dating from the 13th century, were found there when digging on the site, and in 1871 a silver seal was found which bore the name of Isabelle de la Beche.

The poet Lord Tennyson was closely connected with the village; in 1850 he married Emily Sellwood whose home was at Pibworth Manor. Her parents' and grandparents' tomb is inside the railings near the church. His affection for the village was shown when he called his house near Midhurst "Aldworth". Another poet, Laurence Binyon, is buried in the churchyard.

There is a nice little 17th-century inn, The Four Points, very small and rural, and several beautiful thatched cottages. But the magnet that draws sightseers to Aldworth is the collection of brooding stone giants in the church, unique in Berkshire and probably in all England.

Appleton

The village of Appleton, with which the smaller village of Eaton (on the road to Bablock Hythe) has long been associated, stands on a ridge of high ground about 100 feet above the Thames which forms the western boundary of the parish. The name goes back a thousand years; and the woodlands which still partially surround the village reflect a more remote past and the older Saxon name of Earmundslea or Edmund's Clearing. In the present century houses have sprung up along the roads to the north and south, but the old village area, from the Tavern Inn to Charity Farm House, retains much of its former character and charm. The greater part of the present population of about 900 live within this area, which still, however, gives an impression of spaciousness. New, old, and some quite ancient houses co-exist happily in uncrowded proximity.

A few of the thatched cottages date from the 16th century, and the succeeding centuries have all left their mark. It is worth a visitor's while to walk 100 yards down Badswell Lane. He should then cross the main street and go down Church Lane past the Manor pond and tithe barn on the right, the handsome modern school building on the left, to the homely little church with its late Norman arcade and font, which has grown to its present .size and shape through the repairs, restorations and additions of the many generations which have worshipped in it.

The 15th-century tower houses a peal of ten bells, the lantern having been added in 1861 to accommodate the last two. The original peal of six was installed in 1818, an event still celebrated annually on 4th March, and the enthusiasm and competence of Appleton ringers is well known. The rare craft of bell-hanging has been practised in the village by four generations of Whites.

Close by the church is the moated Manor House, one of the oldest continuously inhabited private houses in the country. Like the church, its oldest parts are Norman (about 1190), including a fine rounded doorway and two other Norman archways. Like the church again, it has been enlarged and improved by succeeding generations of owners in the styles of their times, notably in the 16th, 18th and 20th centuries.

Arborfield

Two 17th-century inns mark the centre of Arborfield, on the Reading to Farnborough road—the "Swan", built in 1661, where George III is reputed to have taken refreshment while stag-hunting in 1780, and the "Bull", where Queen Victoria changed horses when visiting the Duke of Wellington at Stratfield Saye.

St. Bartholomew's Church, built in 1863 and a short distance from the village centre, contains the lovely old wooden font and altar rails from an older St. Bartholomew's.

The old "wooden chapel" of Edburghfield, dependent on the church of Sonning, was in existence in 1226, and rebuilt in 1256 of chalk and flint with a wooden tower.

The Infant and Primary Schools share a heated swimming pool; there is one shop and a village hall. A W.I., flourishing Over 60's Club, Young Wives' Group, Gardening Association and a British Legion enrich village life.

While still mainly agricultural, the village boasts specialist craft work—brick and joinery works and two small engineering works.

The village's name is derived from the Saxon, meaning "settlement of Eben or Heben", and in Domesday Book the 60 hides of land and woodland for 300 swine belonged to the Bishop of Salisbury, Lord of the Manor of Sonning. He was supplied with eels from the Mill Pool, which existed on the site of the old manor, later to become Arborfield Hall.

Osmond Bulwe of Edburghfield was the first Norman Lord of the Manor, the name changing to Bulwell in 1331, and in 1590 Thomas Bulwell, owing to an accumulation of debts, sold the estate to Edward Standen for £4,000. Standen built, in 1603, a beautiful manor house designed by the architect John Thorpe.

In Mary Russell Mitford's novel, *Our Village,* the Hall, renamed Aberleigh, is visited by the author in her pony chaise, and Miss Mitford describes it as "a beautiful structure". The Hargreaves and Allbrook families lived in the Hall until the last war, when British and American forces were in occupation. After demolition

5

in 1955/56 the National Institute of Research in Dairying was built on the site.

Part of Arborfield is now War Department property, giving employment to many parishioners. Formerly the Remount Depôt, Point-to-Point races were often held there, a regular rider being the Prince of Wales (later the Duke of Windsor).

Arborfield has changed considerably in recent years. In 1377 there were 29 inhabited houses, 2 uninhabited, 42 families and 171 persons. Today there are many new houses, 1,700 persons, and no daily visit to the village well, fed by natural springs. But one can, like Miss Mitford, still admire the beauty of the River Loddon flowing peacefully along, and like her, lie

"By the smooth Loddon, opposite the high
Steep bank, which as a coronet gloriously
Wore its rich crest of firs and lime-trees, gay
With their pale tassels. . . ."

And when the shadows lengthen on a hot summer's evening, the air scented "with the delicious fragrance of blossomed beans", when the roar of traffic on the high-road has momentarily died away, you can faintly picture a pony chaise bowling happily along the lanes, between hedges "garlanded with woodbine and rose-trees . . .", hear the clip-clop of the pony's hooves, and the happy laughter and chatter of Miss Mitford and Emily, homeward bound from "the old house at Aberleigh. . . ."

Ardington & Lockinge

These two old villages are situated below the Ridge-way a few miles east of Wantage, and are linked together as the centre of the great Lockinge Estate. Much of the 12th-century church at Ardington remains, but it was heavily "restored" in 1847; items of interest are the medieval "squint" in the south of the chancel, and various memorials to the Clarke family who held Ardington Manor for nearly 500 years. The present Ardington House was built in 1719, and is an elegant Georgian building with a splendid double staircase.

The great interest of the twin villages lies in their renown as "model" villages, planned, restored and built by the first and only Viscount Wantage and his wife.

In the mid-19th century Samuel Jones-Loyd, Baron Overstone, came to Ardington with his daughter Harriet, who married Major Robert Lindsay, V.C., of the Scots Fusilier Guards, Equerry to the Prince of Wales. Retired as a young Colonel, Robert Lindsay added his wife's surname, Loyd, to his own, and became Loyd-Lindsay, and later Viscount Wantage.

This remarkable man and his equally public-spirited wife built up the Lockinge Estate over the years, buying in small holdings and houses, and building model houses for their tenants. Old cottages were restored, new houses designed to blend in with the whole pattern, and today it is a pleasure to walk the winding lanes of Ardington and Lockinge.

The gardens are trim, the overall appearance Victorian–Tudor, with steeply pitched roofs and elaborate porches, and a general air of well-being.

The Boars Head Inn, a free house, is a pleasant place to pause, and a great local attraction.

When the philanthropic Lady Wantage bought and restored the inn an old soldier was installed as manager at a fixed salary of £100 a year, plus a percentage of profits from the sale of tea, coffee and hot soup. The profits from the more traditional village pub sales were devoted to building a reading room and installing and maintaining paraffin street lamps.

The Loyd family today lives at Betterton House, originally an Elizabethan farmhouse, now extended and modernised. Visit Ardington and Lockinge in the spring if you want the finest sight of Betterton House, its gardens gay with a million daffodils and cool reflecting lakes.

High on the Ridgeway behind Wantage is the Memorial Cross to Lord Wantage, whose energy, vision and generous spirit invented the villages that exist today.

Ashampstead

known in the 13th and 14th centuries as Esshamstede, is situated on hilly ground in well-wooded country—ten miles from Reading and about nine miles from Newbury.

There is a record of a church before 1086 and the present church of St. Clement dates from the 12th century. Frescoes in the church are of the 13th century, and may have been commissioned from Lyre Abbey in Normandy and carried out by artists sent from there. The wooden bell turret is of the 15th century and the remaining bell bears the inscription "Henry Knight made me 1662".

St. Clement Cottage, next to the church, must go back to the same date as the church—remains of frescoes are of similar nature to those in the church and monks certainly lived there.

Parts of Pyt House, on the road to Bradfield, are of the 16th century with a pastel painted late Georgian façade looking on to lovely gardens. Here, during the past few years, Mrs. Carlisle opened her collection of miniature furnished period rooms to the public in aid of charities. The collection was recently given to the National Trust and is on view at Greys Court near Henley-on-Thames.

Among other old houses in Ashhampstead is the 16th Century Stores, where the sheep clip was sold. This is now a private house and is situated at the cross-roads in the village.

Ashampstead and Burnt Hill Commons lie in the parish. The playing field, "Flowers Piece", was given to the village by Lord Iliffe when the Flowers Piece houses were built.

On Ashampstead Green there are a few cottages and other houses; a Baptist Chapel, now a cottage, was built here in 1840. When a house was built by the Green about 1934 a collection of silver coins was discovered dated in the reigns of Elizabeth I, James I and Charles I.

Ashampstead School, open for almost one hundred years, was closed at Christmas 1971.

The population has risen in recent years and is now estimated at 365.

A monthly news leaflet is distributed in the village.

The main industry is farming with some forestry.

In one of two old cottages (now one house) on Noakes Hill Mr. Noakes lived, and worked close by as a blacksmith. Dog Lane, running west from the cross-roads, is the old road to Hawe and, now a bridle path, is roughly in the shape of the hind leg of a dog.

DOWNS · ASHBURY

Ashbury This attractive downland village, with a population of about 600, is found in the romantically named "Vale of the White Horse"; that oldest of green roads, the Ridgeway, passes above Ashbury, and many are the legends and fantastic stories about this strange and most remote corner of Berkshire. Enclosed by trees to the east of Ashbury is Wayland's Smithy, a burial barrow of the Neolithic or New Stone Age; this tomb lay hidden beneath the earth and sarsen stones for centuries, but was partially restored to its ancient grandeur in the early 1960's.

In his novel, *Kenilworth,* Sir Walter Scott tells the story of the invisible Smith who shoes the horses of wayfarers who leave them overnight at the great barrow, with a silver coin for payment.

Another legendary person connected with this rather eerie part of the county is the magician Merlin, tutor of King Arthur. In a valley behind Ashbury is beautiful Ashdown House, in front of which a great scattering of huge sarsens are said to be a flock of sheep that Merlin turned to stone.

Ashdown House, a National Trust treasure, is a fine Carolean mansion with strong Dutch influence, and was built in 1665 by the Earl of Craven as a home for that beautiful exile, Elizabeth of Bohemia, "the Snow Queen". Unfortunately this sad daughter of James I died before she could make Ashdown House her home.

9

Ashbury is still very much a rural village, but it has one interesting industrial development: a village blacksmith's shop has
grown into a small factory whose road-brushing and snow-plough
products are marketed throughout Europe. At least fifty local
people are employed in this factory. A village which boasts many
fine thatched roofs is lucky indeed to have a resident thatcher, who
is greatly in demand over a wide area.

Things to see in Ashbury: a pleasant small Norman Church, in
the chancel of which the first Sunday School was held by the
Reverend Thomas Stock in 1777; a 15th-century Manor House,
originally owned by the Abbot of Glastonbury; several charming
Elizabethan cottages; a collection of sarsen stones on the west side
of the churchyard which are said to be part of a "mystic circle"
which surrounded the village, much as the village of Avebury is
encircled.

Mystic circle or no, Ashbury is certainly a magical and unique
place to visit.

Within the parish are two small hamlets, Idstone ánd Kingstone
Winslow. At Idstone an attractive 15th-century house is oddly
known as "Trip the Daisy", named after a locally famous coursing
hound whose master was landlord of the old house when it was an
Inn. A painting which hangs in the hall shows "Trip", and under-
neath it hangs a rhyme saying:

> A dog am I as you may see,
> There can no harm be found in me.
> My master he confines me here
> To tell you that he sells good beer.

The parish of Ashbury, Idstone and Kingstone Winslow has
some delightful street and place-names dating from medieval times.
Perhaps the most touching is Roger Page's Lane, named after a
pauper who died "on the parish" a hundred years ago.

Aston Tirrold & Aston Upthorpe The twin Aston vil-

lages merge comfortably at the foot of the Berkshire Downs, and
lie in the valley below the A417 Wantage to Reading Road. The
parish stretches from South Moreton to Lowbury Hill, and houses
about 450 people. The Berkshire Ridgeway lies above it, and Blewburton Hill, an iron-age earthwork to the west, has yielded up Iron
Age, Roman and Saxon relics now to be seen in Reading Museum.

Tradition has it that King Ethelred and his brother Alfred, later
the King, heard Mass together before the first great victory over

the Danes at "Alschendune" on the Downs. A popular belief goes that Ethelred, unready to the last, dithered about in Aston while Alfred went out and won the battle. This is an erroneous legend—it was a different Ethelred from the dilatory King known to every schoolchild. Whether the Mass was held in a Saxon church or the royal tent, it is certain that Aston Upthorpe's All Saints church was built on Saxon foundations, and has an 11th-century nave, a filled-in Norman door, and a 15th-century porch.

St. Michael's church in Aston Tirrold dates back to 1080, was remodelled in the 13th century, and the tower and South Transept added in the 14th century. Both lovely village churches are well worth a visit. The Astons have a tradition of Presbyterianism, and before the Act of Uniformity in 1662, "Meetings in the Barns" were not unusual, and in 1728 the very interesting Presbyterian Chapel was built—one of the oldest in existence in this country.

In recent years there have been many changes in the villages—new houses have been built and the population increased. With the coming of the high-speed train services between Didcot and London more inhabitants travel further afield for employment while those who remain work chiefly on local farms or at the racing stable.

Leisure hours may be spent at either of the two attractive inns—'The Boot' at Aston Upthorpe or 'The Chequers' at Aston Tirrold although a glance at the monthly Village Newsheet indicates how hard many people work to provide interest and entertainment for others and to make the villages happy communities in which to live. The Village Hall, which was completed in 1964, provides an ideal venue for such activities.

Basildon is beautifully situated in wooded rolling country above the Thames Valley, and through the centuries has been variously known as Beorhtel's Hill, Bestleford, Bastedene and Baseldon. An entry in Domesday Book (1086) says, "The King holds Bastedene in demesne. Aileva, a free woman, held it at the time of King Edward . . . in King Edward's time as now it was worth 25 pounds. . . ."

It is now in the "commuter belt" and its worth has improved accordingly.

The Parish Church of St. Bartholomew contains a 15th-century monumental brass to John Clerk and his wife, and in the churchyard is a memorial to the famous agriculturalist Jethro Tull, author of *Horse-hoeing and Husbandry*, published in 1733. The tenor bell, cast in 1621 by Henry Knight, bears the inscription:

In True Desire For to Do Well
The Ladi Litcot Gave this Bell.

The charitable Dame Katherine Lidcott also left in her will (1623) a grant of land in perpetuation of a charity for the poor, which is still administered.

The new and handsome modern church of St. Stephen, built in 1964 with the help of an interest-free loan from Lord Iliffe, is in Upper Basildon. Its ground plan is in the form of that Christian symbol, a fish, and its modern design is of great interest to visitors.

Lord Iliffe, chairman of Coventry Newspapers, lives at Basildon Park House, a fine 18th-century house in classic style; he has been a great benefactor to Coventry and its cathedral, and also to the villages of Basildon and Yattendon.

This village is full of interest for the visitor: at the beginning of this century the eminent architect Sir Edwin Lutyens, designer of New Delhi, made good use of the local brickworks when building some village cottages at the request of Major Morrison, who then lived at Basildon Park.

On the site of the old brickworks now stands the Teneplas factory, one of the most modern plants in Europe for making extruded plastics, whose cables are laid under seas and across deserts, notably the Capetown/Lisbon/London telephone, repeater tube, sections of which lie in places three miles down on the sea bed.

Kenneth Graham wrote his famous *Wind in the Willows* about the stretch of the Thames along the Basildon reach, and his beloved Rat, Mole and Toad lived along its banks.

Mr. Gilbert Beale, who died in 1967 at the age of 99, created a riverside park with a pavilion, a peacock farm, sculptures, fountains and water garden, and left it for public pleasure under the Child-Beale Trust, now associated with the National Wildlife Trust.

Basildon has its ghosts . . . Lady Fane, who lived in that splendid house called The Grotto, was found drowned in the well within the house, and her unquiet spirit is alleged to haunt the building. There are two other Basildon ghosts . . . Nobes-on-his-white-horse, who lived at Tomb Farm, and Nan Carey, who was believed to be a witch.

Who has not heard of Basildon Bond? This popular writing

12

paper is named after this Berkshire village. In 1911 the head of the firm of Dickinson was staying at the Park as a guest of Major Morrison, at whose suggestion the new paper was christened Basildon Bond and sent out to success all over the world.

The village today consists of about five hundred houses, some old and many relatively new. It is beautiful and well-cared-for, sophisticated rather than rural, charming to look at and a pleasant place to live in or to visit.

Harley Wood is still gay with bluebells in the spring, and the initiated know where to find the woolly thistle, the bird's-nest orchid, and the unfortunately named stinking hellebore.

Beech Hill

The village of Beech Hill, thought to have formerly been Beche Hill after the de la Beche family, has little easily discovered history, because a fire destroyed most of the archives prior to 1860.

Between 1142 and 1184 Jocelyn, Bishop of Salisbury, confirmed the grant by William de Stuteville, Lord of the Manor of Stratfieldsaye, of the Hermitage of St. Leonard of the Loddon. The hermitage became the property of the Benedictine Abbey of St. Mary of Vallemont prior to 1260.

A copse surrounded by a moat is the only evidence left of the Castle of Beaumys, lying to the east of the priory of St. Leonard, castle and priory belonging, by 1272, to Hugh de Spencer, who was deprived of them later by Edward I.

In 1444 Henry VI gave the Hermitage of Stratfieldsaye and Stratfield Mortimer to Eton College.

Beech Hill House was built by the Harrison family in 1720, and bought by the local land-owning Hunter family, whose connections with Beech Hill originated in the 14th century.

A daughter of the Hunter family, Mrs. Forbes paid for the building of the church, consecrated in 1867, and, on her request, moved from the Winchester to the Oxford diocese. She and her daughter also built the vicarage and endowed the living. The church was "densely crowded" for the consecration ceremony and afterwards a Wellingtonia tree was planted in Beech Hill House grounds and the parishioners "partook of tea round it".

The school was built in the mid-19th century by the Duke of Wellington, the number of pupils varying at first from 18 to 70, accommodated on long benches and in a gallery above the schoolroom. Children stayed at school until they were 14 till just before the '39 war. One of the headmistresses, Miss Hughs, attended as a pupil, and told of the times all the children had to parade once a

13

week in a circle in front of the Headmaster with their slates, and when he shouted a number they had to write it down. As they passed him he gave them a "terrible clout on the shoulder" if their work was wrong. Her mother used to pad the left shoulder of her dress to give her protection, but they soon learnt their numbers!

The school inspectors must have been a terrifying experience for teacher and child alike, more so because teachers were paid according to the number of pupils that could read. In one case the year's salary amounted to £19 5s.! A report of one inspection reads:

"H.M. Inspector, the Revd. C. D. du Pont. 25 children over 6 years of age. The examiner expressed himself much pleased with the progress made in the last year. [Vicar's note] *n.b.*— The children behaved very well. Inspector's manner in examining the Holy Scriptures very flippant and unpleasant. . . ."

The Jubilee reservoir was built in 1897 to commemorate Queen Victoria's Diamond Jubilee. The original pump had broken down and the well was full of muddy surface water. Donated by Mr. J. J. Ratcliffe, the reservoir held 16,000 gallons of water, thus giving the village a magnificent supply. All was not well, however! In 1905 the tap would not work, and nobody seemed to know whose responsibility it was to repair it—eventually a 1d. rate was charged for its maintenance. In 1907 it started to leak copiously— a £25 County Council loan and local subscriptions remedied it. There was back-biting too, as a motion was passed that people outside the parish couldn't draw water unless they paid maintenance; this was a pointed dig at the Queen's Head public house, which although attached to the village, is actually in the next parish. A later meeting allowed the publican to use the water.

In 1937 a severe drought dried up the reservoir, and water from an imported tank was sold off at 1d. per pail. The "mains" reached Beech Hill just in time for the outbreak of war, but the ornamental railings that had adorned the reservoir were turned in as "war effort".

Sadly, the village school is now closed, but the village green, which had deteriorated into a head-high jungle, has been cleared, flattened and re-planted, and a few swings put up in the corner. The duck pond has been cleared and cleaned. The population is around 400.

There is a regular daily bus service (when it comes), and only two houses remain unconnected to the new main drains. Progress is relatively gentle in these parts!

Binfield

To the hurrying motorist, the Binfield part of the busy A329 provides access to the M4. It is possible to take a more leisurely route, B3034 from Windsor to Reading, but there will be few who know that they are using the old Turnpike Road created in the 18th century so that wheeled traffic could journey more comfortably along the Forest tracks. The formation of the Turnpike Trust to build the "Forest Road" is commemorated by an oval stone set up by the road side at Bill Hill. Windsor Forest covered all this area and was well stocked with fallow deer for the King's hunting. The severe game laws pressed heavily on poacher and peasant alike to maintain the royal prerogative.

Binfield derives its name from the coarse grass in this clearing or "feld" in the forest. At one time the forest was divided into 16 Walkes. The Binfelde Walke was mentioned in the 16th century under Sir Henry Neville, the keeper, who lived at Billingbear, a huge Tudor mansion, now pulled down.

The centre of Binfield is only 2½ miles from the rapidly growing town of Bracknell, but the village remains rural, surrounded by carefully farmed lands. Woods with anemones, bluebells, and primroses are easy to find. Magnificent great oaks stand in the middle of the village, which is long and straggling (4½ x 2 miles), running along a ridge that is 260 ft. above sea level. To the north is the old parish church of All Saints, and to the south Amen Corner. The corner is said to have taken its name from the congregation of a Dissenting Chapel, built in 1875, who used to say to each other as they separated after a service, "God be with you, Amen". There are glimpses of the Chiltern Hills to the north-west, and to the east, at night, golden lights float soundlessly to earth, winking from planes landing at Heathrow, 15 miles away.

Until recently a flourishing brick and tile works at Amen Corner employed 60 craftsmen making fine, wire-cut bricks.

Beehive Lane is clearly named from the old brick kilns. Conveniently near The Royal Standard in the middle of Binfield is the old Working Men's Club, active since 1906. The Memorial Hall next to the club was erected by public subscription and opened in 1920. The football and cricket clubs share the spacious recreation ground, and the August visitor will enjoy the annual carnival which displays its attractions for a whole week, ending its jollifications with a grand procession that parades hilariously through the length of the village.

No large-scale industry is to be found in Binfield, as it has become largely residential. Binfield Park, a fine Georgian mansion built in 1729, is now a hospital for the handicapped. Newbold

College, a growing concern, is a training college for Seventh Day Adventists. Binfield Lodge, one of James I's hunting lodges, claims that Elizabeth I slept there and boasts that Cecil Rhodes was one of the visitors. Elm Grove in Monk's Alley has a raised bowling green, which may have been the site of ancient earthworks. White Hill, the erstwhile home of Alexander Pope, is now called Pope's Manor. It has been greatly enlarged since the youthful poet wandered through the woods, a lonely Catholic outcast. Binfield Place is said to be the oldest house in the village with a history that goes back to Henry VII. It has 16th-century moulded beams and a chimney marked 1702. Bad luck will befall the owner if a 17th-century bas-relief of a lady's head is moved.

Of the many Inns, the most interesting is the Stag and Hounds, on the Forest Road. It was converted into an Inn in 1727. William Cobbett described an excellent breakfast he had there on his way to Reading. Outside was a venerable elm tree, said to mark the centre of old Windsor Forest.

The parish church of All Saints has been much restored, but the main part dates from the 14th century. There is, however, a record of a priest of Binfield as early as 1174. The unusual open wooden porch, with different carvings on both sides, is 14th century, and there is some fine 15th-century glass. A unique hour-glass stand of hammered ironwork beside the pulpit, dated 1628, is worth attention. The half-length brass memorial to Walter de Annefordhe in the chancel, is one of the earliest in Berkshire. Both the Queen and Princess Margaret have worshipped here, when staying in the neighbourhood.

The Rectory has a long history. It was enlarged in the last century probably to enable the rector, the Rev. Gabell, a retired headmaster from Winchester College, to take in pupils. Constable sketched some of the elms and Sir Beerbohm and Lady Tree were among the famous guests who stayed there. It has now become an expensive ancient monument and is no longer the focal point of the village, so a new rectory is going to be built more in the centre.

The churchyard of All Saints has become a wild flower sanctuary. At least 23 different species grow here and all can enjoy the snowdrops and primroses that carpet the ground, and the smell of the sweet-scented roses. Birds, too, nest and sing undisturbed. Saint Mark's Church, at the other end of the village, is a Chapel of Ease built in 1867. It has been recently rebuilt after a fire destroyed it in 1958.

Bisham If you are lucky enough to come by water you will find this gem of Thames-side villages just beyond Marlow. There is a church tower, a cluster of red roofs, the great house which is Bisham Abbey, and behind it all, woodlands and hills . . . Ashley hill, Speen hill and Applehouse hill.

In the days when the Thames was both waterway and highway, this was how the world came to Bisham, and the names of the visitors over the centuries read like a drum-roll of English history.

The Templars had a small community here, and later William de Montagu, Earl of Salisbury founded a priory, to which was brought the body of Warwick the Kingmaker, and later that young Earl of Warwick executed in the Tower by Henry VII. Margaret Pole, Countess of Salisbury, lived at Bisham at various times, before she too fell victim to Tudor savagery in the Tower.

The magnificent house that is Bisham Abbey today was built by Philip Hoby, trusted servant and ambassador of Henry VIII. He bought the Priory and land from the Crown, beating Anne of Cleves to the bargain.

It is a Tudor mansion of the Renaissance, preserved today as a Grade I listed building, and one of the architectural treasures of Berkshire.

Sir Thomas Hoby, younger brother of Philip, inherited Bisham Abbey and lived here with his formidable wife Elizabeth . . . one of three Cooke sisters who greatly influenced society in their day. One married Sir William Cecil, and was the mother of Robert Cecil, Queen Elizabeth's secretary, and was founder of the great Cecil dynasty. The second Cooke sister was the mother of Sir Francis Bacon; the third, Elizabeth, married first Thomas Hoby, and after his death, Lord Russell of the Bedford earls.

At beautiful Bisham everyone of importance was entertained . . . all the Cecils and Bacons, the Seymours, Lady Katherine Grey (sister of Jane), Elizabeth the Queen and most of her favourites, James I and his Queen.

If you visit the church today you can see the wonderful Hoby Tombs, among the most celebrated in the country. They are beautifully carved, coloured and gilded, the kneeling figure of Elizabeth Hoby, Lady Russell, dominating them all. Her daughter, Bess Russell, is there, with her two little girls, and Sir Philip and Sir Thomas lie side by side in gilded alabaster armour.

There is a story that Elizabeth Hoby beat her little son so severely that he died, and all because he had blotted his writing book. Certainly Elizabethan parents were, by today's standards, cruel to children; and certainly the little Hoby son died at an early age. Look at that alabaster face in the church, and decide for yourself. Local legend has it that the Abbey is haunted by her repentant spirit.

Today it is owned by the Sports Council, who have built an indoor Sports Centre in the grounds. The old Abbey itself is superbly maintained as an administrative building and is, perhaps, a memorial to the last private owners, the Vansittart Neales, whose two grandsons were killed in the Second World War.

Bisham is rich in atmosphere, architecture and history—a place to explore.

Blewbury

The Icknield Way runs from East Anglia to Salisbury Plain, and where the A417 cuts it on the Berkshire Downs you will find the lovely village of Blewbury.

If you are wise you will park your car and go on foot, because the village has grown up within four encircling roads round a network of streams and footpaths. Only the visitors with time to wander and loiter will see the real village of orchards, old houses, ancient thatched walls and waterways. King Alfred's great battle of Ashdown was fought near Lowbury Hill, at the junction of the Blewbury, Aston Tirrold and Compton boundaries in an area named in the Domesday Book as "The Hundred of the Naked Thorn". In Saxon times Grim's Dyke was dug across the downs, parallel to the Ridgeway, and local legend has it that the devil ploughed it in one night, creating two large mounds with the scrapings of his plough and a clod he threw at his imp for driving a crooked furrow.

A plaque placed on Churn Nob records that St. Birinus preached to the heathen from this spot in 634 A.D.

According to Domesday Book, Blewbury was divided into three manors: one for the King, the second for the Church, the third belonging to the Count of Evreux. This last was known as Hall Barn or Nottingham Fee, and both these names survive in Blewbury houses today. Hall Barn, which changed hands repeatedly through hundreds of years, was a hunting lodge for Henry VIII, and the home of the Fuller family in the Civil Wars. During restoration work this century a document was discovered hidden in a wall and proved to be John Fuller's oath of allegiance to Oliver Cromwell, carefully hidden from Cavalier eyes. This harassed gentleman is known to have entertained both warring factions on the same day, and descendants of the family had a service of pewter and a tablecloth used for both sets of compulsory guests.

Blewbury has several inns worth visiting—the Red Lion, the

oldest; the most amusingly named, The Load of Mischief; the New Inn, once the Blewbury Inn and later the King William, once had a sinister reputation for robbing and murdering travellers, who were then buried in the orchard, and a new fruit tree planted on each grave.

A famous miser was Vicar of Blewbury from 1781 to 1824— one Morgan Jones, known as Blewbury Jones the Miser. The coat he wore was patched till not a shred of the original remained, his wardrobe generally was "borrowed" from scarecrows, and he always visited parishioners at mealtimes to get a free meal. When he died in his native Wales, he left an estate of £18,000, a large sum in the early 19th century. He is the original of "Blackberry Jones", the character created by Charles Dickens in *Our Mutual Friend*. Blewbury has always attracted artists and writers—Luke Fildes, Blandford Fletcher and T. F. M. Sheard all painted village characters. Novelists Marguerite Steen, G. B. Stern, Barbara Euphen Todd and Dick Francis are residents, and Kenneth Graham of *Wind in the Willows* fame lived here for some years. A pleasant modern housing estate is named after his much-loved book.

Steve Donaghue once trained horses in Blewbury, and the famous Ribero is only one of many winners who excersied on the gallops above the village.

Things to look for in Blewbury: A fine Parish Church, with hagioscopes (or squints) cut in the west piers to enable worshippers to see the altar; and notable memorial brasses to Sir John Daunce, surveyor to Henry VIII, and Dame Alice Daunce. The Malthus Charity School, a beautiful 18th-century building still in use as the infants' school until new buildings were completed in 1971; a wealth of lovely old cottages as fine as any in Berkshire; a cottage picture gallery and antique shop where local artists and potters show their work.

Blewbury is a very old place, but its spirit is young and adventurous. It has a good Village Plan to preserve its amenities, it produces plays and pageants and makes music; it supports numerous societies and clubs; and on each Christmas Eve the Blewbury Mummers present their medieval Mummers' Play at public houses round the village.

19

Boxford is a picture-book village of immense charm, resting comfortably in the Lambourn Valley with the little brimming river running between the beautiful cottages.

Take your camera when you visit here . . . there are photogenic gems in all directions.

Outstanding among the old houses is Boxford Mill, built across the Lambourn River to the rushing mill weir. The gardens are gay and brilliant, and from the little bridge leading into the heart of the village there is a perfect view. At any time of the year travellers will be found leaning on the bridge to look at, and photograph, Boxford Mill.

This village is as old as it is beautiful . . . there are signs that the Romans cut a way through the forests here to Speen. Katherine of Aragon was granted lands at Westbrook by her faithless Henry VIII, and both Cromwell and Charles I rode over the ford at Boxford during the Civil Wars.

The Church of St. Andrew, beautifully set among thatched cottages in the centre of the village, was ancient when it was restored in the 15th century; there is a Saxon chancel, traces of an early fresco of the Ascension, or Christ in Glory, and a fine pulpit with a splendid tester or canopy. St. Andrew's Church in 1534 had one of the first three English Bibles in Berkshire. The very capacious church porch used to be the site for the swearing of oaths.

A huge elm, known as the Clerk's Tree, which marked the centre of the village where three roads meet, unfortunately suffered Dutch Elm disease and was replaced by a Windsor Oak to celebrate Queen Elizabeth II's Silver Jubilee in 1977. Where the steep lane climbs over the hills to Winterborne lie the grounds of Boxford House. Built on rising ground and with a magnificent view over the Lambourn Valley, this is a handsome stone house which used to be the old Rectory when it was built about 100 years ago, in a late Tudor style. A large wing was added at a later date, and when the whole thing became too vast for any clergyman to keep up, a new rectory was built near the church.

At the gates of Boxford House is an attractive old lodge, in its day the original rectory of the village. Opposite the lodge is the cottage where Oliver Sansom, the Quaker, lived in the 17th Century. It is known as Oliver's Cottage, and remains much as it did in his day.

The people of Boxford are rightly proud of their beautiful village, and a resident, Mrs. Elsie Huntley of Heather Pine, Boxford, has written and published an admirable and scholarly history of this delightful corner of Berkshire, called *Boxford Barleycorn*.

Bradfield The original village of the Broad Field, with church, mill and manorial Bradfield Place (remnants now incorporated in the College), stands around the Pang chalk stream, noted for its Blue Pool a mile or so up stream, where springs keep the sandy bottom fuming with miniature volcanoes, while a trick of light in the transparent depths produces an intense blue. These springs have never failed, even when droughts have dried out the upper reaches of the Pang.

The 7th-century royal charters quoted by Abingdon Abbey's *Chronicle* suggest that there may have been some temporary grant of land here to that Abbey at the time of its foundation. But apart from a delightful legend of Bradfield monks sallying forth to oppose a detachment of William the Conqueror's army approaching from Theale, and the survivors being suffered to retire to the mother house at Abingdon, there is no word of any monastic site. The so-called Monastery Wall, with Tom o' Bedlam's Hole, are relics of a much later Bradfield Place.

Domesday Book makes clear how deplorably Saxon Bradfield had wilted in twenty years under its new Norman master. Yet two hundred years later the manor was among the wealthiest of twelve held by the lords of Dudley, when it passed to the De la Beches of Aldworth, which may account for the similarity of the 14th-century workmanship in the nave arcades of both these churches.

For three centuries the history of the nation left little mark here until, in October, 1644, a letter to the Parliament announced that "My Lord General quartered all night at Bradfield. . . . Great bodies of the enemyes Horse are in view, but whether to face or engage we know not".

How thankful the villagers must have been when the Second Battle of Newbury was done with and the fighting moved away northwards. The Parish Constable's Accounts at that time give a sad picture of the disruptions and exactions endured at the hands of Cavalier and Roundhead alike.

During this 17th century the importance of Bradfield's Rectorship brought to it John Bowle, who at the same time was Dean of Salisbury and Bishop of Rochester, succeeded by Richard Bayley, Charles I's chaplain and President of St. John's College, Oxford. Bayley was ousted under the Commonwealth by the sensational John Pordage, in whose time there were very queer goings-on at the Rectory, which became troubled with hordes of spirits, among them a huge fiery dragon with a tail eight yards long, which engaged the Rector in combat for several hours on end!

Elias Ashmole, whose wonderful collection formed the nucleus

21

of the Ashmolean Museum at Oxford, came to Bradfield at this time, bent on marrying the rich widowed lady of the manor, despite the attempt of one of her sons to murder him. The unhappy couple (she was twenty years his senior) soon moved up to London, leaving Bradfield Place to decay. All was sold to a London merchant, who built himself a brand new mansion which has totally disappeared, leaving its name to Great House Wood and its site carpeted with snowdrops.

Bradfield Hall was then built in 1763/4 for the Hon. John Barrington, natural son of George II. His successor presented the parish with the block of four two-storey almshouses that bears his inscription of 1811.

But the vital history of Bradfield began when the manor came into the possession of Henry Stevens, whose great-grandson, Thomas, was to change its face completely. This remarkable man dominated the local scene for nearly half a century after becoming "squarson" in 1842. He virtually rebuilt the 14th-century church, one of Gilbert Scott's first commissions, of which he always felt specially proud. With the idea of founding a choir-school for this enlarged church, Thomas Stevens opened a school in what remained of Bradfield Place. The school grew rapidly, as new buildings were added year by year. Amongst other activities the founder was a pioneer of steam-ploughing and milking machines; he also started a mineral water factory at St. Andrew's Well. An authority on the Poor Law and contributor to its reform he was instrumental in establishing the local Workhouse, which now functions as a hospital for mentally handicapped women and children. Unfortunately his energies and enthusiasms were not controlled by financial judgement, so that his many activities led to his being declared bankrupt. Since he was by far the largest landowner and employer in the parish, a great deal of hardship ensued. His College, however, had been taken over by a Governing Body, and has gone on growing in size and reputation, famous for its Greek theatre.

Meanwhile the parish has also increased and prospered, developing right away from the old village (which has become largely College property, including its one haunted house) on to the higher ground at South End. Although the total area of alluvial valley and plateau gravel supports some sixteen farms, its agricultural labour force has thinned away. The great majority of the present inhabitants are employed outside the parish, except for a recent development of joinery works.

Busless on Sundays, South End has had to be provided with a

church of its own. And the primary school, whose 1866 premises in the village were long ago relinquished to the College, is also at South End, as are the village hall, playing fields and social club. There too stands a most impressive war memorial. Its exceptionally fine setting was designed by George Blackall Simonds, the name of whose only son is among those inscribed on it.

In the old village the outstanding addition has been a restoration and expansion of the riverside group of Old People's Homes, which is an absolute masterpiece.

Most recent innovation of all, the M4 has sliced the parish in two with its lordly swath commanding the finest scenery for miles around, but taking trouble to treat rights of way with proper respect. A few footpaths have been lost, out of the large number possessed by this parish and jealously tended by its Parish Council.

Among unusual names are: Scratchface Lane and Honey Bottom. The old village has no inn at all, the nearest being a good mile and a half away.

Bray Everyone who has enjoyed singing "The Vicar of Bray" will have heard of this village, made famous by its vicar, Simon Alwyn, who changed his religion three times, rather than surrender the living. It is happily situated at a bend of the Thames, a mile from Maidenhead. Bray is derived from the Saxon mean-

23

ing "a moist place". It is an enchanting village within easy reach of London, an advantage that the Hind Head, in the middle of the High Street, has fully realised. It is now a restaurant famous for Old English Fare. We are told it was originally built to house the stonemasons building the church.

The church of St. Michael dominates the village, but though it dates from Edward I it has been much restored by Victorian architects and only the Perpendicular tower remains to remind us of its long history. Within the church are many beautiful and elaborate brasses, 14th, 15th, and 16th-century examples. There is an alabaster monument to William Goddard, a member of the Fishmongers' Company, and his wife Joyce Mauncell. William died in 1609 leaving instructions in his will for the building of Jesus Hospital, in Bray High Street. There was to be a chapel and 40 alms-houses surrounding a garden courtyard. These most attractive old houses have been modernised and the visitor will not fail to notice them, as there is the white figure of the founder in a niche over the entrance.

Chauntry House (originally a Chantry Chapel), near the church, erected in 1753, has a varied record. It has been a workhouse, an infirmary, and at one time a local jail. There are many Elizabethan houses scattered about the village and every effort is being made to keep alive the character of the rural community.

Brightwell-cum-Sotwell

Just outside the boundary of historic Wallingford there has been a settlement since the 10th century—Beorthanwille, Shottanwille and Maccanie are still there and flourishing, but today we call them Brightwell, Sotwell and Mackney. In Domesday Book, 1087, the Lord of the Manor is given as the Bishop of Winchester. The fine old church of St. Agatha at Brightwell is built on ancient foundations, but is mainly 12th-century transitional with 14th-century additions. The 12th-century tower was rebuilt in 1797. There are three fine 16th-century memorial brasses; that dedicated to John Scoffyld, 1507, in the south aisle, is remarkable as the only instance in the county of an effigy of a priest holding the host. Another brass commemorates Robert Court and his wife Jane, 1509, who lived at Sotwell House in the reign of Henry VII, and entertained that Prince Arthur whose death cleared the way for Henry VIII. A third brass shows Richard Hampden and his wife, 1512; the first entry in the parish register is 1564.

The Chapel of St. James, Sotwell, was almost entirely rebuilt in 1884, but much of the 14th-century roof was retained, as well as the foundations and a small 12th-century window in the north wall of the chancel.

The population of Brightwell-cum-Sotwell stood at 234 souls in 1676, and today numbers something over 1,538. There are eight charities in the parish, which provide for the relief of poverty, for apprentices, free teaching, and for "the binding out of poor children born in the parish".

Brightwell has some interesting Churchwarden's accounts, which tell that in 1709 three masons were paid 9 shillings for two days' work; at the coronation of George II the Churchwardens provided the village with cake, drink and cheese at a total cost of 26 shillings.

An interesting sidelight on the government's efforts to bolster up a failing wool trade is shown in the 1680 record which states: "Catherine Wiggins of Sattwell made oath that Mary Webb was buried in woollen only, according to the late Act of Parliament, before Richard Skinner, Mayor of Wallingford".

Brightwell is an attractive village to wander in, with many beautiful old houses and cottages of architectural or historic interest. Sotwell House is moated and Tudor in origin, Brightwell Manor mainly Georgian; Brightwell Priory and the Abbotts House were probably part of a monastery; Dobsons is an old Tudor House, and Small's House, an Elizabethan building until recently owned by New College, Oxford, is thought to have been a Bishop's Palace.

The village almshouses, built in the last century by Edward Fairthorne, were let in 1927 for 6d. per week.

Brightwell-cum-Sotwell has a rich accumulation of songs, rhymes and mummers' plays, many still remembered and sung at Christmas, May Day, and Shrove Tuesday. Among many Berkshire versions of the Shroving songs, surely this is one of the most jolly:

"Pit pat the pan's hot
And I be come a' shroving,
Cast the net before the fish,
Something is better nor nothing.
A piece of bread, a piece of cheese,
A piece of apple dumpling.
Up with the kettle and down with the pan,
Give me a penny and I'll be gone!
Give me another for my little brother,
And we'll run home to Father and Mother."

One hopes they got their pennies . . . and that many visitors will discover for themselves the variety and charm of Brightwell and Sotwell.

Buckland Here is a delightful stone-built village which looks north across the Thames Valley to the Cotswolds, and south over the Vale of the White Horse to the Berkshire Downs.

It is rural and agricultural, many of its 500 inhabitants working elsewhere, or in the serenity of retirement. The beautiful Manor, Buckland House, is owned by Mr. Richard Wellesley, but used as a University Hall for 140 students taking London University degrees.

The original Manor was granted to Hugo de Bocland in 1229, and afterwards held by Thomas Chaucer, son of Geoffrey Chaucer of the *Canterbury Tales*, father of English poetry. Under the Tudors it passed to the Yate family, then to the Throckmortons, that great Roman Catholic family who contributed so much to 16th and 17th-century English history.

The present Buckland House was built in 1757, with a park of noble trees, a herd of fallow deer, and a fine heronry.

There is a Norman church to see, an ancient mulberry tree in the Vicarage garden, under which, it is claimed, Charles I rested during the Oxford period of the Civil War.

Buckland is small but lively . . . it has a school, a village hall, two shops, an inn, a children's swimming pool, numerous clubs and social activities, and a bus service to Oxford and Swindon. As well as the old Anglican church, there is a Roman Catholic and a Baptist church, and the ruins of a Baptist Dipping Well.

Bucklebury & Marlston The village of Bucklebury is small but the parish of Bucklebury and Marlston is scattered over several miles of Common, an area of great natural beauty, and the home of foxes and badgers.

From Westrop Green to the Avenue is about five miles, and the original splendid oaks are thought to have been planted to commemorate a visit by Queen Elizabeth I to the Manor. Others were planted in the 18th century and another row added to celebrate the victory of Trafalgar.

There are some beautiful Tudor cottages and farm houses tucked in among the trees, and Bucklebury claims to have more footpaths than any other parish in England.

The great Common was once enclosed by gates to prevent straying cattle, but now only the names remain . . . Nuttage Gate, Hatch Gate, Brown's Gate and Vanners.

Like many Berkshire villages, its origins are Saxon, and the earliest Charter of 956 records that King Edwig granted wood from Hawkridge for rebuilding the church at Abingdon.

A church already existed and Bucklebury belonged to the Crown in the Domesday survey, and Henry I granted the Manor to Reading Abbey early in the 12th century. The Abbot's five fishponds can still be seen today.

After the Dissolution of the Monasteries, John Winchcombe, son of the rich woollen merchant Jack o' Newbury, was granted the Manor by Henry VIII, and built a fine Tudor mansion on the site of the Abbot's house.

The male line of Winchcombes died out in 1703, and the Manor passed to Frances Winchcombe, who married Lord Bolingbroke. At the Manor House the Bolingbrokes entertained Dean Swift, Alexander Pope and John Gay, and many other notables including, it is said, Queen Anne herself. Despite great social success, the marriage was an unhappy one, and Lady Bolingbroke died in 1718, a broken-hearted woman. Her ghost is said to drive through the village in a coach drawn by four black horses, and on one night of the year she sits in the drawing-room of the Old Vicarage.

Bucklebury is rich in hauntings . . . an evil spirit is said to way-lay nocturnal travellers and chase them down the Devil's Steps. What is described as "a grisly apparition" appears in broad day-light on the isolated commonland called Bushnell's Green; a lady in white flits along the Avenue at Beenham turning, and two monks have been seen near the medieval fishponds on the Common.

The psychical researcher should have plenty of material to work on at Bucklebury.

The Manor House, enlarged by Lord Bolingbroke, was destroyed by fire in 1830, leaving only one wing, the kitchens and the dovecot. This wing was restored in recent years, and is the home of the present Lord of the Manor.

St. Mary's Church, a Saxon foundation with Norman, 15th, 16th and 17th-century restorations, is well worth a visit. The south doorway is Norman, 1150–1160, the Tower 15th-century, with interesting figures on the south-east buttress; the eight bells date from 1581, and a chancel beam is inscribed '1591 Francis Winchcombe Esq. built this". A stained glass window dated 1649 shows a crest, a sundial and a fly . . . to remind the passer-by that time flies!

The famous artist, Sir Frank Brangwyn, designed the five modern windows in the chancel and a north window in the nave.

A little chapel still in use is called Morton's Chapel and has an interesting story. In 1835 Parliament proposed to enclose Bucklebury Common, and a wayside preacher called John Morton went to London, courageously opposed the bill, and was successful. He returned to his preaching in an old blacksmith's shed at Bucklebury, was ordained a Pastor of the Congregational Church, and succeeded in building a new chapel at a cost of £400. This is the chapel you can see today.

Other things you should not miss in Bucklebury and Marlston: a medieval barn and waterwheel on the River Pang; the old foundry dated 1717, whose registers give fascinating details of rural economy before the Industrial Revolution; the Blade Bone Inn, so called because the copper sign reputedly encases the blade bone of a mammoth from pre-historic times; the Pot Kiln Inn, near the old brick and tile works; Chapel Row, scene of the old country fairs; Coronation Oak, where the Coronation of Edward VII was acclaimed before 1,200 people by the Rev. Cecil Hope Gill.

The Marlston Church was largely rebuilt in the 19th century, but retains a Norman doorway, and flints used to face the outer walls came from a Roman site at Wellhouse.

Don't miss Merry Tidbury's beech tree by Fanny's Road. A reveller returning from a convivial evening at the local inn tied two beech saplings together, and they have grown into a single tree with the knot clearly visible.

The whole area of this ancient parish teems with history, legend, natural beauty and mellow man-made places of interest.

Burchetts Green

from the Saxon Byrchehurste (hurst meaning copse) is a small village with a population of about 400. Many of them work in Maidenhead or commute to London. The village stands rather uneasily astride a busy main road connecting two even busier trunk roads, the Maidenhead–Henley and the London–Bath roads. The houses edge the Common and the Green, or straggle along the main street, and are surrounded by woodlands, fields and farmsteads. It has no parish church divided as it is between the three ecclesiastical parishes of Stubbings, Hurley and Littlewick.

Stubbings Farm, in the centre of the village, boasts a barn reputed to be 400 years old, and old maps mark Stubbings Heath to the south. It is believed that the road through the village was made by Lord Salisbury, for his personal use. As his health was poor he journeyed from his home at Hatfield to take the cure at Bath, and went this way to avoid the highwaymen lurking on Maidenhead Thicket. The milestones on this stretch give the distances to these two towns. "Alleyhill Coppes", now Ashley Hill, dominated the scene then as it does today.

Woodlands Cottage, 17th century, was formerly a Quaker Meeting House. It stands next to a house which was formerly the village bakery, run by Horace Lowe. His speciality was lardy cakes and the children on their way to school would pop in for a quick warm-up. The school, a Church of England Primary School, was built in 1868 on land conveyed by deed poll by Sir Gilbert Gilbert-East. Facing the Green stands the Crown Inn (mentioned in 1847), and in modern times is a very worthy prize-winner in the competition for the best-kept public house. Stubbings House, half a mile to the east of the village, was the home of Queen Wilhelmina of Holland during the last war when her country was invaded by the Nazis.

The noble manor house of Hall Place is now taken over by the Berkshire College of Agriculture. It is approached by a magnificent avenue of limes. It is recorded that Hurley Priory owned Hall Place, until the dissolution of 1535. In 1728 it was puchased by William East of the Manor House, Kennington, who pulled down the old house and built the one standing today. It remained in the family until after the last war, when it was sold to the Berks. County Council. The old mansion stood in a great deer park of some 130 acres. Descendants of this herd now roam wild on Ashley Hill. Interesting out-buildings include a bee-house and an ice pit, and in the gardens can be seen the remains of a cock-fighting ring.

Various monuments to Lord Nelson existed at one time, such as a statue of him overlooking the Park, and it is said that the oak trees there were planted in the formation of the ships at the battle of Trafalgar. One of the fields is still named "Nelson's". The re-building necessary to accommodate the students of today was done with the greatest care so as to preserve wherever possible the 18th-century decorations.

Among the legends and ghost stories of the neighbourhood is that of Claude Duval, the famous highwayman who is said to have carried out his expeditions in this area. Both Woodlands and Burchetts Green House are said to be haunted, the latter by Druids! Hall Place is no exception and students claim to have seen a coach and horses crossing the lawn at the back of the house. The ghost of a coloured servant has also been seen at Black Horse Lodge. More recent anecdotes of the Clayton East family include their driving to Ascot in their horse-drawn carriage and, if the day had been profitable, scattering their winnings to the servants lining the drive, on their return. It is also said that unless Sir Gilbert could see across country to the spire of Shottesbrook Church the gardeners were in trouble for not keeping the trees trimmed back.

Within living memory a well in the centre of the village supplied the villagers with water, geese grazed on the Green and an old warhorse was tethered there, a far cry from today's busy restlessness.

Burghfield

In the reign of Edward I, Matthew de Bergefield, moved with pity for the peasants who had to cross the marshy flats of the Kennet to reach Reading, built a narrow bridge across the water for them to pass in safety. There had been many accidents, and the Abbot of Reading, to whom the land belonged, would do nothing to help them. Later, de Bergefield widened the bridge for carts and men on horseback to be able to pass.

In the time of his grandson, Peter de Bergefield, the King commanded the bridge to be repaired, and Theobald le Carpenter, who was presumably the King's steward, tried to compel Peter to contribute to the cost. He refused, saying that the building of the bridge had been an act of grace on his grandfather's part, therefore his heirs had no liability. A jury was appointed to try the matter—but no record has been found of their verdict.

In Burghfield Church are two alabaster monuments of immense historical interest. The recumbent figures have recently been definitely identified, by means of their armorial bearings, as Richard Nevill, Earl of Salisbury, born about 1400, and Alice, or Eleanor, his wife. The eldest son of this pair was Warwick the King-maker.

It is difficult to account for the presence of these effigies in Burghfield, though a local legend has it that they were dragged by galloping horses from Newbury, and that the complete erasure of the lady's features is due to her having turned over en route!

It seems more probable that they were brought by some means —galloping horses or no—from Bisham Abbey, the foundation house of the Nevills, Warwick the King-maker himself being buried there. Perhaps the effigies were removed to this remote village for safe keeping at the time of the dissolution of the monasteries.

The wooden effigy of Roger de Burghfield was moved, when the church was rebuilt in 1843, from its original place in the chancel, to a dark corner under the belfry stairs. It was identified at the same time as the alabaster Nevills, and was restored to the chancel, a special oak sarcophagus being made for it.

A skirmish of undecided results, between Prince Rupert's cavalry and the Roundhead forces then lying at Newbury, was fought at Burghfield Bridge.

Birchbroom making was a former Burghfield industry, and farming always was, and still is, the chief local occupation.

Until recently, mummers performed their ritual play, "St. George and the Dragon", at the Three Firs Inn, but this custom ceased when the inn was demolished—just one more rural "memory" to be passed on to younger generations.

Calcot

The small village of Calcot, about three miles west of Reading, sprawls in rather an amorphous fashion around the A4, the old London to Bath road, and originally formed part of the Manor of Tilehurst.

The Manor was sold in 1604 to Sir Peter Vanlore, a Dutch banker and moneylender. Four years later James I made grants to him of the fee farm rents with a water-mill, rights reserved by the Crown.

In 1706 the Manor was in the possession of Benjamin Child, the husband of Mary Kendrick, one of the family of noted cloth merchants in Reading, and heroine of the ballad, *The Berkshire Lady*. This poem relates that at a wedding party, Mary Kendrick fell in love at first sight with Benjamin Child; failing to attract the shy young lawyer's attention, she sent him an anonymous letter asking him to meet the writer in the Park. Arriving with a friend at the appointed spot, Benjamin was confronted by a masked and armed lady, who challenged him either to marry or fight her, giving him half an hour to decide. After consultation with his friend, Benjamin chose the former; luckily the marriage is said to have been entirely successful. After Mary's death, Benjamin Child sold the Manor to John Blagrave, who pulled down the Vanlore house and built the existing Georgian mansion, now a golf club.

Early in the present century, Calcot Park was let by Mr. Harry Blagrave for a short period to Lord Northcliffe of the *Daily Mail*. A test run had been arranged for motor cars, from London to Bristol and back; motoring was still in the experimental stage. On arriving at Calcot, the entrants were entertained to breakfast by Lord Northcliffe. Only a few cars succeeded in completing the return journey.

Calcot boasts what must surely be one of the strangest tombstones in the country—a memorial to alcohol—erected on what was once a cob-nut nursery and apple orchard, lying adjacent to the estate of Calcot Green, owned by Colonel C. B. Crabbe.

31

About a hundred years ago, so the story goes, the nursery was managed by an eccentric Quaker-like gentleman called Mr. Webb. Although in his time he had been fond of a glass of wine, he finally turned against drink and decided to dig a grave, in which he poured all the wine and beer that he possessed. At its head he erected a tombstone, on which were written the following lines, which made up in fervour what they lacked in true poetry:

Beneath this stone lies buried
Our race's deadliest foe;
Myriads he has hurried
Down to the realms of woe.
More mischief he produces than filled Pandora's box,
And more disease produces, than plagued the Egyptian flocks.
Evils attend his reign,
Yet thousands own his sway,
And madly hug the chain
That drags their souls away.
Reader, beware his wiles, he lurks within the bowl,
And stabs you while he smiles, then oh! shun alcohol!

Miss Gertrude Jekyll, the renowned landscape gardener, describes in her book, *Wood and Gardens,* a visit she made to the cob-nut nursery in the late 19th century. Mr. Webb, dressed in his old-fashioned black clothes, showed his visitor the fine Hamburg vine, the cob-nut trees, the especially large daffodils, and, lastly, with pride, the tombstone erected in memory of his alcoholic past. Miss Jekyll was much impressed.

If one takes a stroll down an inviting footpath leading off the Bath Road, one is very soon confronted by the desolate, neglected remains of a vast apple orchard. The tombstone is still there, though now standing in a cottage garden, and the lettering well-nigh indecipherable, but it is not difficult to imagine the stern, erect figure of the sombre clad Mr. Webb striding between the trees.

Though only a small hamlet, Calcot is in two parishes; on one side of the Bath Road in Theale, on the other side in Tilehurst.

Now increased by ribbon development but still not large, the inhabitants vote for and are represented on two parish councils, and vote in two County Council divisions.

California covers part of the parishes of Finchampstead, Barkham, and Wokingham Without. At the turn of the century most of the land was included in the Bearwood Estate, owned by the Walter family; the Nine Mile Ride just one ride of many through Windsor Forest. In 1924 six estate cottages were the only dwellings between Park Lane and the California cross roads, surrounded by open country, bracken, heather and silver birches, and well-known for its population of adders!

Many trees were felled by Canadian troops during the first World War, but John Walter had already planted the famous Wellingtonias and other trees in the Nine Mile Ride area.

One of a few lodges on the Ride was called California Lodge, and the land round was marked as "California" on an old map. This was the origin of the name.

After the 1914–18 War all the land was put up for sale to meet heavy death duties, occasioned by two deaths in the Walters family. Prices were incredibly cheap—10s. per foot for frontage plots, and back acreage almost thrown in. Even by 1930 a plot, 80 ft. x 200 ft., could be bought for £80. An article in the weekly magazine *Titbits* helped sales by describing the healthy life in this new paradise—children swung from tree to tree like young Tarzans, and slept on pillows stuffed with dried pine cones; rabbits and pheasants abounded, and horse-riding was universal. The article did not, however, mention the lack of shops and buses, absence of piped water, gas or electricity, and the poor soil.

Much of the land was sold to ex-servicemen, health damaged by war, who, unable to find employment in London, envisaged earning a living raising poultry and families in healthy surroundings. But in the early '30s tariffs on feeding stuffs and rising prices forced many farmers to sell up.

Early building was haphazard and of poor quality. One house was built completely in a tree, with access by rope ladder, the owner claiming that as there were no foundations he should not pay rates.

Over the years residents had used Longmoor Lake for bathing in summer and skating in winter. The area was bought by a Feltham garage owner named Cartledge, who ran mystery evening coach tours to the lake. This proving popular, he built a small shop and café, later a dance hall and children's amusement park, and by a stroke of genius called it "California in England". In a good summer 1,500 children a day enjoyed the model railway and show-boat, and the "California Poppies" speedway team gained fame. Gradually the name California was adopted by the whole

33

district, and the County Council agreed to the name on signposts and Post Office.

In 1926 residents decided that a centre must be provided for growing families. With help of a loan from Colonel St. John of West Court, the West Court Club Hut was built, under the organization of retired schoolmaster Mr. Woods. Local lads painted, decorated, equipped it, and laid out a tennis court and football pitch. Dances were held, and a drama group and other activities begun. All seemed set fair—then a split on future policy. Mr. Woods wanted the lads to start levelling ground for a bowling green, but after much long, hard work the boys not unnaturally wanted to enjoy a season of arranged football matches. Persistent arguments resulted eventually in the club closure, and sale of fitments to repay the loan. The County Council bought the building for a school for local children, rebuilt as the Nine Mile Ride Primary School after the war.

A resident well remembers that up to 1927, a large notice alongside the old brick kiln on Kiln Ride read "WARNING, MAN TRAP".

St. John's Church was built in the early 30's to serve the needs of the rising population.

California is here to stay.

Caversham Park

No quaint old cottages, no ancient inns, no village pond, or elderly residents who remember "the good old days in the village"; for this is a new community. It is only a few years since the first road was cut through the rolling green acres, and the first houses appeared rather self-consciously above the Reading–Henley road.

Nevertheless, Caversham Park is achieving its own very real personality, the houses are mellowing, the trees growing gracefully and the residents have every right to be proud of their "village". Do any of them stop to think of the colourful events connected with those once rolling acres? Do they picture the grazing deer, the terraces, the fountains and winding drives? Do they tell their children tales about the great house, the visits of Elizabeth I, captive Charles I and Oliver Cromwell? As the men-folk plan the lay-out of their gardens at weekends, do they perhaps feel the reassuring presence of gardener-extraordinary Capability Brown who, in 1761, laid out the grounds of Caversham Park for Lord Cadogan?

Walter Gifford, relative of the King, was Caversham's lord when Domesday Book was compiled. His possessions descended to William Marshall, Earl of Pembroke, who was Regent during the minority of Henry III and who died at Caversham Castle in 1219. William's five sons were successively Earls of Pembroke. Richard, Earl of Hertford, inherited after the Pembrokes, but, disliked by the King's foreign favourites, he was poisoned,

Anne, daughter of Richard Beauchamp, subsequent lord of Caversham, became wife of the great "King-maker" Earl of Warwick, who died at the battle of Barnet, and mother of Richard III's Queen.

The royal manor was granted in 1493 to Notley Abbey, Bucks—only a moat and all within it reserved for the King. After the Dissolution the manor passed in 1542 to Sir Francis Knollys, who enjoyed high royal favour, except during the reign of Mary, when he fled to Germany. His wife Katherine was first cousin to Elizabeth and she remained with her aunt, Anne Boleyn, during the unfortunate Queen's imprisonment and execution. Knollys had custody, at Bolton Castle, of Mary Queen of Scots, and later urged her beheading.

In 1601, his son Sir William was lavish host to Queen Elizabeth at Caversham, where also in 1613 he received Queen Anne of Denmark, consort of James I, on her journey to Bath—no doubt to "take the waters".

Charles I found shelter here, during the Civil War, and was prisoner within its walls in 1647, when he wrote seeking re-union with his children—a meeting which Cromwell, a spectator, is said to have considered most touching. The mansion was later wrecked in the fighting.

That great military leader Lord Cadogan, who succeeded the Duke of Marlborough as Commander-in-Chief, purchased the estate in 1718, demolishing the old war-scarred manor house and building, by 1723, a mansion of great grandeur set in the midst of a vast formal lay-out of drives, terraces, fountains, parterres and statuary, of which the most dramatic feature must have been the two 900-feet-long canals with a Doric portico at each end. In the words of that architect of great houses, Colin Campbell: ". . . this noble Lord, from a place that could pretend to nothing but a situation capable of improvement, with vast labour and expense, has now render'd it one of the noblest seats in the kingdom . . .", praise indeed from one who ought to know!

Campbell's "Geometrical Plan of the Park, Gardens and Plantations of this magnificent Place" shows the mansion to have had frontage of some 300 ft.—only 20 ft. shorter than the garden façade at Blenheim, which perhaps Cadogan was seeking to rival. Cadogan is said to have spent £130,000 on Caversham, and this at a time when he had only recently been forced to repay a debt of £30,000 to the Duchess of Marlborough. Financial catastrophe is believed to have overtaken the noble Lord in the last years of his life, and the house and estate probably passed into the hands of his creditors on his death in 1725. Certainly there is no mention, in his will at Somerset House, of the Caversham estate.

Five or six years after his death, a letter from his brother and successor at Caversham Park, Lord Cadogan of Oakley, showed that the creditors were still pursuing the family, and were preparing to cross to Holland and proceed against Cadogan property there.

The debts were eventually paid, for Cadogan remained the owner of the Park for 50 years. His wife was the daughter of Sir Hans Sloane, and it was through her that the Cadogan family's Chelsea properties came into their hands.

It was during the ownership of their son, Charles Sloane Cadogan, that "Capability" Brown remodelled the grounds in his characteristic fashion, removing what traces survived of the formal lay-out of 1723. Tradition has it that the mansion was partially destroyed by fire in Cadogan of Oakley's time, and this is substantiated by the diarist Mrs. Lybbe Powys, who noted, in the 1770's, that the mansion then in existence was much smaller than the earlier house. A contemporary couplet indicative of the standing of Caversham Park ran:

"At Blenheim, Croome and Caversham we trace Salvators' wildness, Calude's enlivening grace. . . ."

In the early 1780's the estate was sold to a Major Marsak, recently retired from service in the East India Company. Mystery surrounded the gentleman—believed by many to be a natural son of George II by the Comtesse de Marsac, a lady of Hugenot descent who had come over with the Hanoverian court; and no doubt his arrival in the district set tongues wagging in many withdrawing-rooms!

His son and successor in 1820 suffered heavy gambling losses, and forced him to take refuge from creditors on the Continent, all the furniture and fittings of the house being sold by public auction six years later.

A wealthy iron-master, William Crawshay, lived in the greatly embellished Marsack Mansion until 1850, when, with the exception of the still surviving colonades, the house was totally destroyed by fire. As befitted his trade, Crawshay rebuilt the mansion about an iron frame, giving it a strong, solid character. He had the good fortune to reach the zenith of his powers when the early railways were being developed, and were ready to use his iron, and he was worth nearly £2,000,000 when he died in 1867. His son Robert carried on the family business at Cyfarthfa, near Merthyr Tydfil, and his son, then his widow, were the last private owners of the estate, in 1921.

From 1922 to 1942 the Roman Catholic Oratory School (now at Woodcote) occupied the house. In the following year it was taken over by the B.B.C., who to this day run a monitoring station there, keeping check of the entire world.

The Estate Bell is still in position behind the old brick walls—but the gardens have been made into a caravan site, and men tend their own beans, not "the Squire's"; the mansion still overlooks a charming lake—but instead of "My Lady and her tea guests", typists and telephonists sit beside it; instead of the deer, there are children playing; instead of a coach and four, there are minis and motor bikes and boys delivering the *Evening Post*.

Caversham Park has changed—but it is very much still alive!

East Challow

This small village at the foot of the Downs lies on the Faringdon Road just west of Wantage, and has a population of about 1,000. The last few years have brought many changes . . . the winding road has been widened and re-routed to take the increasing traffic, new estates of houses have sprung up, and two new schools have been built.

Once completely rural and agricultural, the villagers now mainly work at Oxford, Harwell or Wantage, and of five windmills mentioned in earliest records only the memory remains in the name Windmill Hill.

There are two old public houses, one attractively placed on a small green off the busy road. The Goodlake Inn until recently had been run by the Lovegrove family for 130 years.

In the centre of East Challow are several charming old cottages, and the church, although much restored, has some interesting sights for the visitor. There is a tub-shaped Norman font, some 13th-century arches, the low arcade with capitals only shoulder high; and an unusual old lectern of a black eagle fighting a serpent. Above the beautiful carved wood chancel arch is the figure of a knight in armour and a woman in a wimple.

The only industries in East Challow are a small factory making wooden farm implements, and a foundry about 100 years old whose front offices were once an old coaching inn.

Beside this building the old Berks. and Wilts. Canal used to run, but, like many another waterway, it no longer functions.

West Challow

This White Horse Vale village is well off the road from Wantage to Faringdon, so has retained its rural charm and resisted the more blatant assaults of progress. It is a settlement of great age; at Cornhill Farm the remains of a Roman villa were excavated in 1876, but sadly, not preserved. The site has been ploughed over, but the outline of the villa is clearly visible from the air. The usual coins, tiles, nails and fragments of pottery have been dug up over the centuries.

In 1950, when mains sewage trenches were dug, a skeleton was found in an old cottage garden, and the site of a very early Friends' Meeting House and burial ground established.

West Challow was once two manors—Petwick Manor, granted to the nuns of Amesbury, and the Manor of Challow, given by Henry I to Richard Acland between 1107 and 1118.

St. Lawrence's Church is a good example of a simple village church, with a 12th-century nave, 15th-century chancel with the original window, and a fine 14th-century bellcote. There are two bells, the treble being cast by Paul the Potter, a London bell founder between 1283 and 1312, which makes it possibly the oldest signed bell in Berkshire. The inscription reads: PAUL LE POTER ME FIST.

The second bell was cast in 1629 by Ellis Knigh 1st, in Reading, and the church register dates from 1653.

Another "oldest in Berkshire" that West Challow can claim is a fine old thatched cottage . . . old and new are comfortably blended in a very pleasant village.

Field and farm names are full of character: The Marsh, Bug's Island, Garland's Hill, Common Ground, Maze Hill, Coppice Leaze and The Stitches; and near West Challow a few rare wild flowers are just holding their own—the Wild Tulip, Greenwinged and Early Purple Orchids, and the Lesser Periwinkle.

Charney Bassett

On the banks of the River Ock, about eight miles from where it joins the Thames at Abingdon, sits the small and very rural village of Charney Bassett. It houses about three hundred people, has one small post office stores, a village hall, a public house, a primary school which is shared with Lyford and Denchworth, and very little public transport.

But it is strong in antiquity and peaceful charm, and in the Middle Ages lived under the wing of the great Benedictine Abbey of Abingdon. Charney Manor contains some of the most beautiful medieval buildings in England and was originally a grange of the Abbey. The house now belongs to the Society of Friends and is used as a meeting-house, conference centre, and residential hotel.

Cherbury Camp, within the parish of Charney, is a prehistoric earthwork of great interest, constructed on the pattern of hill-forts like Uffington Castle, but it is located in flat marshland.

Legend says that King Canute had a palace at Cherbury, but there is no evidence that this unlikely site once boasted anything so grand. However, Canute legends persist around Charney Bassett, so possibly the Great Dane at least visited the neighbourhood.

The delightful name Charney Bassett comes from two sources— Charn, a Celtic name for the River Ock, and the Norman family of Ralph Bassett, who died in 1127 and held land in the district.

Visit, if you can, the church of St. Peter's, Charney; it is a wonderful survival of a small, early Norman parish church, probably built on a Saxon foundation, and the centre of life for generations of people for a thousand years.

Lyford

Across the River Ock from Charney Bassett, and in the same ecclesiastical parish, is the hamlet of Lyford. The name, of course, derives from a ford over the river, and the Ly (or in an older form, Lin) indicates a place where flax was grown or retted.

Lyford's link with the great pageant of history lies in Lyford Grange, the house where the Jesuit priest and martyr, Edmund Campion, in the reign of Elizabeth I, was captured after celebrating Mass, in 1581. He has now been canonised.

The small church, mainly Jacobean but built on the site of an earlier oratory or chapel-of-ease, serves a parish of only seventy souls. Lyford has neither shop nor inn, but shares all the amenities of Charney Bassett across the river.

Chieveley

The wild chives that grow profusely all around this lovely downland village have given it its name. Chieveley lies about five miles north of Newbury, just off the A34, but the coming of the M4 with an interchange point near Chieveley has now brought great changes to this gentle and rural settlement.

Walk along its main street and you will find many beautiful cottages and several notably fine large houses of Queen Anne and Georgian architecture. A lovely Regency verandahed house behind high walls has particularly fine gardens, and is modestly called

39

"The Cottage"! The Manor House looks out over superb views of the rolling Downs towards Winterborne.

Once a self-sufficient village with shoemakers, wheelwrights, blacksmiths, bricklayers, carpenters, an undertaker, and a shop "that sold everything", Chieveley now follows the prevailing pattern . . . the craftsmen have mostly gone, but there are two good food shops, a butcher's, a Post Office, and a doctor's surgery with a group practice of three doctors.

There are three public houses, and one, the Hare and Hounds, has a clientele from all over the north of Berkshire, who visit the famous old skittle alley.

On the outskirts of the parish is the Blue Boar Inn, a free house and a most lovely thatched building that sits high on the Downs with magnificent open views towards Newbury. The inn sign, a life-size stone Blue Boar, is alleged to have been brought by some of Cromwell's men from Yorkshire, and left at the inn when they camped on North Heath.

The planners have done well in Chieveley, leaving the old centre of the village virtually intact, but building considerable new housing in estates to the north and east of the place. There is a fine village hall with playing fields, and a great number of community interests and social clubs.

With a beautiful rural setting, good shopping at the nearby market town of Newbury, and fast access to London by motorway, Chieveley is a village which combines most of the advantages of the modern world.

Childrey

Here is a beautiful village to visit, lying below the line of the Downs between Wantage and Ashbury, in the Vale of the White Horse. It is green and peaceful, with several very beautiful houses near the church, some fine old cottages, a village pond to delight the painter or photographer, and the tranquil air of being just off the beaten track. The name Childrey comes from CILLARITHE, that is a stream rising in the village that belonged to Cilla, who was sister to the first Abbot of Abingdon in 673. There were once three manors here: Freethorne, now vanished; Rampagne, the home of the Fettiplace family, where King Charles I spent a night in April 1644; and Maltravers or the Old Manor, named for the family who lived there about 1300.

In the Old Rectory garden is a magnificent cedar tree with a trunk 27 feet round, grown from a seed brought from Aleppo and planted in 1646 by that great Arabic scholar, the Reverend Edward Pococke.

Good old street names are Stowell, Dog Lane, Horse Road, Rotten Row and Round Town, but the last name has been unimaginatively altered by the Council to Chapel Way.

Some field names have not been tampered with—Little Onions, Cotstile and Charnhill are pleasant examples.

Childrey is very much a rural village. Older inhabitants have kept their Berkshire dialect words, which add a little colour to our increasingly flat, uniform, telly-conscious speech. Here are a few for collectors: Pooter (to cry), Snook (stole), Crope (crept), Slammocky (untidy), Dout (put the fire out), Shucketty (shaky), Chopsing (being cheeky), Frum (firm), Unked (weird), Tarblish (tolerable), Pikked (pointed) and Deedy (careful).

MORE BERKSHIRE DIALECT WORDS—Thick Caddle (chaos), There then I (There I was then), Arthurt (across), Spwoort (sport), Bottom (a valley), Butt (A piece of land shorter than a furlong), Quabb (boggy land), Stabble (to kick mud about the house from muddy boots), Shard (a stile), Wuut (a mole), Vorights (opposite), Peg Muzzle (a gate an animal can't push open), Where's the old buoy? (an "old buoy" is always a child or teenage boy, never a parent), Louze (verb) (to turn cattle out to grass), Louzy (noun) (a meadow or pasture).

Chilton

Sited 400 feet above sea level but built in a small valley in wide downlands, the village of Chilton (population 1,000) lies just below the A34 on the opposite side to the Atomic Energy Research Establishment.

In a countryside rich in Bronze Age, Celtic, and Roman remains, the ancient settlement is first mentioned in King Offa's document as Ciltinne; King Edgar (970 A.D.) granted lands to the Abbey of Winchester, and Edward the Confessor recorded two Manors held by Wenric, Place Farm and Manor Farm. Both these names exist in Chilton today.

Domesday Book (1086) assesses the little place at "5 hides supporting 2 manors and 7 villeins and 9 bordars with 1½ ploughs outside the demesnes". Cromwell's army passed through Chilton and destroyed the church tower; the railway came through Chilton to Newbury in 1879; a bomber command airfield was built in 1940, and the A.E.R.E. came to the parish in 1946.

With such a rich history, Chilton is an interesting village to visit. Let us take a tour of the village.

Entering from the Didcot-A34 road, one comes first to Manor Farm. The church sits above on the right, and is a Norman shell with many additions and restorations. It contains an interesting

41

nine-sided font, the tower and porch are Victorian, and the six bells are dated 1623, 1665, 1770 and 1892, which last is also the date of the clock. Embroiderers will be particularly interested in the kneelers, beautifully designed and made by villagers, all with some reference to Chilton life and interests.

The Old Rectory is now divided into three, the middle residence probably dating from the 16th century. Opposite is an old timber and brick house called Goddards after the family who lived there through the 18th and 19th centuries.

Below Goddards is the old School House (1860) and opposite it the remaining two wings of Lattons Place, now called Place Farm.

Outside Place Farm stands the village pump, the centre of life until after the last war, when piped water arrived with A.E.R.E.

Down Main Street are several fine old cottages and the village shop. At the Rose and Crown Inn one can turn left up South Row to Downland Nurseries, one of 14 or 15 commercial orchid-growing concerns in the country. This nursery has achieved world recognition as British specialists in Lady's Slipper Orchids.

There is a tiny Primitive Methodist Chapel in South Row, built in 1855 but no longer used.

If you turn right at the Rose and Crown you will reach the A34 via Major Bewicke's training establishment, where about 35 fine steeplechasers are currently in training. One of the local sights is the string of horses crossing the A34 to train on Chilton Mile along what the locals call Chilton Bottom, parallel with the Ridgeway and Grim's Dyke . . . which brings us back to prehistory.

The church records are worth looking at, and the spelling in the 18th-century Overseer's Accounts something of a collector's piece. The Overseer looked after "the pore" and paid out "for altren the surplis, 1/-,' for "a new brom, 1/4d.; "spent at the Visitation for eating and drinking 15 pepal—15s./9d."; "for 2 botels of wine and 2 pene loves, 6s./2d."; "paid a seman—2d."; "gave to 11 men disabled by the Turks, 1/-".

You will enjoy a browse around Chilton. On its outskirts are a number of new housing estates, many connected with the Atomic Energy Research Establishment, which employs a large proportion of Chilton people. Their children are fortunate in that the excellent A.E.R.E. school on the site comes within the Chilton parish.

Cholsey

The name Cholsey is thought to have evolved from the Saxon "Coel's Eye" . . . Coel was a Saxon King and Eye means island. The land hereabout is marshy and still has a drainage problem, so the settlement was most likely on an island near the Thames. The prehistoric road called Icknield Way crosses the River Thames at Cholsey.

In the 18th century this village boasted a population of 200; today it is about 5,000 with signs of continuous growth. There are some delightful thatched cottages, one still called the Old Bakehouse, but much of Cholsey is recent estate building.

The pride of the village is the Church of St. Mary, built on an earlier Saxon foundation in 1130, and mainly of stone and flint; the beautiful chancel is often described as the finest in a Berkshire village church, while the Sanctus Bell is the second oldest, being cast in London by Richard de Wimbish between 1290 and 1310.

Henry I gave the church to the Abbots of Reading, who also had a summer residence at Cholsey.

The old parchment Parish Register dates from 1539, one year after Henry VIII ordered that every wedding, christening, and burial be recorded. In 1540 Alyce Wyllmott, daughter of John Wyllmott, was baptized . . . and there is still a member of the Wilmot family living in Cholsey. A beam in Lollingdon House is carved John Wilmot, 1516. This historic house was also the home of the late poet laureate, John Masefield. Take the footpath from Cholsey to Aston Tirrold to see Lollingdon House. There are fine walks all around Cholsey and a bird sanctuary between Bow Bridge and the River Thames. Kings Standing Hill, Unhill Bottom, Lollingdon Hill, the Lynch Banks and the Fair Mile are all areas of outstanding natural beauty.

Time marches on . . . the Wallingford Road Railway Station, built for the Great Western in 1840, is now the Berkshire Downs Café! The handsome Cholsey Viaduct, a pleasant feature in the Thames Valley landscape, was designed by that "little giant" Isambard Kingdom Brunel. It is good to reflect that his genius is being properly appreciated in the latter half of this century, before the bulldozers of Progress demolish what remains of his work.

A bridge over the railway connects two large expanses of open fields . . . perhaps this is why it is called the Silly Bridge.

The green in the centre of the village is called the Forty, and it is thought that this derives from the forty paces of archery.

Look in at the Vicarage garden and you will see two splendid monuments to human frailty. The Reverend Wyatt Cottle, vicar from 1801 to 1832, honeymooned at Mount Lebanon, where his wife coveted the famous Cedars of Lebanon. So she smuggled two tiny trees into England in her parasol, and there they are today, growing in glory in an English garden.

Cholsey is full of interesting things to see . . . the blacksmith's shop in Honey Lane now makes wrought iron work, and in the same lane the Beehive public house is appropriately named. Fairmile Hospital, the old Berkshire County Asylum, sits in beautiful grounds laid out by Sir Joseph Paxton, who designed the Crystal Palace Exhibition of 1851. There are many rare trees here, notably a fine Tulip Tree and a Maidenhair Tree, from Western China.

A bell is rung at the Forty by a local resident, to bring in the New Year ; and the handbell ringers of Cholsey made their London debut at Heals department store in 1968, ringing Christmas carols and tunes. In 1971 the Cholsey Scout Troup got into the *Guinness Book of Records* for a pram-pushing marathon. A new sports pavilion with spacious changing rooms was opened in 1970; a great many money-raising activities have paid for the strengthening of the old church tower, and for refitting new frames for the ancient bells. The work is now complete, and once again the bells ring out over Cholsey and the Thames Valley.

Cold Ash

is a straggling village rising to over 500 feet above sea level, and although it can boast no particular beauty spots, there are many pleasant walks, especially fine woodland walks and glorious views across the Pang Valley on one side, and Wiltshire and Hampshire on the other, perhaps the most varied and beautiful country within reach of Newbury.

In Fence Wood are remains of the outer ramparts of the prehistoric camp, called Grimsbury Castle, and in the same wood, a timber platform of an ancient dwelling, assumed to be of the same age. The ramparts, though much overgrown, are still quite perceptible. In the centre of the old camp stands a curious little castellated cottage with a peaked roof.

It was from Cold Ash that the Parliamentary Troops, led by the Duke of Manchester, marched from Clay Gill and through Ashmore Green, to launch their attack on Shaw House in the second Battle of Newbury. This attack finally forced King Charles to abandon Newbury and take flight. It is said that Red Shute Hill was so called because it was red with blood during the Civil War.

The Church of St. Mark was built by C. N. Beazley, 1864-5, and is of brick with bands of stone and vitrified bricks. It has a polygonal apse, and an unusual stone pulpit with geometricized flowers. There is some good stained glass by Clayton and Bell, also by Kempe, 1891. The old school is being replaced by a modern building in three stages.

St. Mary's Nursery is owned and run by the Church of England Children's Society.

Downe House, a large public school for girls, came to Cold Ash in 1921 from the village of Downe in Kent. The building was erected during World War I for a religious organisation known as the School of Silence.

Many of the older buildings in the village have recently been demolished. The best known to older residents are: Collaroy House, formerly the home of the Rev. Bacon and his daughter Gertrude, pioneers of ballooning; the Old Shop House, one of the earliest village shops; the Children's Hospital which stood on an original ox-road between Wales and London. The hospital site was a halting-place where the animals were milked and the milk given away to the villagers. The well at which the animals were watered has recently been filled in.

The recreation ground, between the wars, was cleared of gorse and heather and began to take its present form. Most progress has been made during the past ten years, for before this, the grass was cut only once each year by tractor and farm mower.

The village hall was erected in 1926 with money raised in the village. The pavilion and committee room were added in 1957 with the aid of voluntary labour. There are many clubs and organisations in the village for recreation. The Miniature Rifle Club, now extinct, was one of the oldest, and regularly competed at Bisley. For the young there are the Playgroup, Sunday School, Cubs, Brownies and Guides. There is a Square Dancing Group, football and cricket clubs. The Horticultural Society was founded well over forty years ago. For the ladies of the village there are Women's Institute, Mothers' Union and Floral Club and the Evergreen Club for the older members.

Coleshill

Choose a sunny day to see this loveliest of Berkshire's old villages. As the name implies, it is built on a steep, winding hill, and its immaculate stone houses stand at odd angles and levels, making beautiful patterns of grey roofs and walls and little lattice windows.

In all directions are rolling green hills and valleys, magnificent trees, and the tranquillity that most of our countryside has lost.

Local legend insists that the name derives from Old King Cole of the nursery rhyme, and Cole's Pits is the site of the one-time merriment and fiddling. The Earls of Radnor owned Coleshill House, which was built in the 17th century by the Pratt family, allegedly to the design of Sir Roger Pratt, the plans being revised by Inigo Jones. It sat in magnificent parklands and was completely destroyed in a tragic fire in the 1950's. The National Trust keeps a watchful eye on the entire settlement, so Coleshill need not fear the ravages of the developer.

There is a charming square towered church about half-way down the hill, set above the road and behind a small village green, with magnificent views out over the valleys. On the day of our visit a few children were kicking a football about the Green, and the church was locked. Picturesque the churchyard certainly is, with tombstones leaning in all directions.

Like most of old Berkshire, Coleshill has a long history. A Priory once stood here before the dissolution of the monasteries, the land afterwards bought by a London merchant, Sir Henry Pratt. The family was for the King in the Civil Wars, and Charles II "received and borrowed" one hundred pounds from Dame Margaret Pratt.

Another local family, the Pleydells, followed the Pratts; Pleydell-Bouverie is the surname of the Earl of Radnor; the little village public house is called the Radnor Arms.

When you visit Coleshill, take the A420 from Faringdon to Swindon, and follow B4019 on the outskirts of Faringdon through some of the loveliest unspoilt countryside in the county.

Compton Set in the folds of the Downs on the old railway line from Didcot to Newbury, the village of Compton has seen many changes over the centuries. The Hundred of Compton is called Nachededorne in Domesday, and the beautiful little village church, flint walled and sturdy, still retains some Norman features. The lower part of the tower is transitional Norman, there are four transitional arches, and a simple Norman font. The chancel has been beautifully decorated and there is a peal of six bells. Authorities seem to be unsure whether the church is dedicated to St. Mary or St. Nicholas but it is well worth a visit, and is situated about a quarter of a mile out of the main village on the way to Pangbourne.

There are some attractive old cottages, and a fine village inn, but Compton generally wears a 20th century face, with large new housing estates and a very good community hall with adjoining playing fields.

On the road out towards Hermitage a large modern school caters for children from a wide catchment area.

Farming is still a major way of life, and racehorses are trained on the Down above the village. Children are everywhere to be seen . . . the quiet Downland village must indeed be a splendid place for children growing up.

Cookham consists of three main areas: the village of Cookham, Cookham Rise and Cookham Dean. The name seems to have a Saxon derivation meaning simply "The home of the Cook". There is also Cookham Hundred spelt "Cokham Hundred".

Cookham is situated on a particularly beautiful curve of the Thames under the famous Cliveden Woods and beside the riverside meadows of Cockmarsh (owned by the National Trust). It is bordered by agricultural land to the west, east, and south, with the river on the north. Cookham village is linked to Cookham Rise by a narrow strip of road known as The Pound, which adjoins Cookham Moor, also National Trust property.

The old pack-horse track from London to Oxford crossed the river at the Lady Ferry (no longer in use), traversed Cookham Moor, continued through Cookham Dean, and recrossed the Thames between Bisham and Marlow. Cockmarsh and the Moor are favourite picnic grounds, with the nearby sailing clubs providing interest for the spectators. Odney Common is popular with the children, being bounded by the mill-stream and a quiet backwater where they can fish; or if they have ponies there is plenty of room to ride.

The High Street is noted for the unusual number of different types of architecture used for the houses and yet blended together to make a fascinating whole. Many of the older houses are listed of historical and architectural interest. The parish church of Holy Trinity is of great historical importance as it is almost entirely Norman. Fine monuments, ancient brasses and the famous picture by Sir Stanley Spencer depicting "The Last Supper" adds to its interest.

Sir Stanley was born and bred in the village and some of his paintings are on display in the little Spencer Gallery not far from the church.

During the present century, the Cookhams have attracted an artistic and literary community especially among the younger generation. Sculptors, artists, dramatists, writers and musicians all find encouragement in Cookham. Every other year "The Cookham Festival" is held, which takes its place with other important centres, providing an outlet and stimulation for creative work.

Every July the "Swan Uppers", in their bright red jerseys, come to sort out the swans on the Thames. Since medieval days the swan has been considered a royal bird, and no one can own a swan without royal permission. Many of the London Guilds used to share this privilege, but now only the Dyers and Vintners claim this honour. The Swan Masters nick the beaks of the cygnets, the unmarked birds remaining the property of the Crown. This ancient ceremony stems from the time when the Guilds undertook to raise and maintain companies of bowmen for the King's defence.

Most of the recent building development has taken place in Cookham Rise. The railway station is the focus for the new Council Estate and shopping precinct.

Great Coxwell

Not far west of Faringdon and just off the Shrivenham road lies the little village of Great Coxwell. It is a quiet place of narrow lanes and old stone cottages with bright gardens; very old, very peaceful. There is some new housing at one end of the village, an attractive church, a small village hall. But the glory of Coxwell is the Great Barn, a superb medieval tithe barn that attracts visitors from all over the world.

In the early 13th century the Cistercian Abbey of Beaulieu had a cell at Great Coxwell, and the Great Barn was built. It is made of Cotswold stone, its massive buttresses faced with ashlar, roofed with stone tiles, and truly noble dimensions . . . 152 feet long, 44 feet wide and 48 feet up to the ridge.

The structure is so strong and durable that most of the building is original and well cared for today by the National Trust, who publish an admirable leaflet giving information on the history and architectural details of the barn.

After the dissolution of the monasteries the Great Barn passed to the Mores family, and in the 18th century to the Playdell-Bouveries, and later to Mr. E. E. Cook, who bequeathed it to the National Trust.

Cranbourne The parish of Cranbourne has been formed comparatively recently, cut out of the parishes of Winkfield, Old Windsor and Sunninghill. The Gothic Victorian Church, built by Benjamin Ferrey in 1850, is of flint and stone. It was dedicated by Bishop Wilberforce, who argued fiercely against Darwin over the *Origin of Species,* and was known unkindly as Soapy Sam. Some of the stained glass windows are designed by William Morris. The Alexander Chapel is in memory of Field-Marshal Earl Alexander of Tunis, who died in 1969. His house was not far from the church where he worshipped.

One of the oldest schools in Berkshire was founded at Cranbourne in 1709 by Richard, 1st Earl of Ranelagh for 'twenty poor Protestant boys and twenty poor Protestant girls'. It became known as the 'Green School' as a uniform rather like the more famous Blue Coat School was provided for the children. Every Whit Monday they paraded outside Winkfield Church to receive a new set of clothes. The number of admissions increased over the years and in 1880 a larger school was opened in Lovel Road called Winkfield Cranbourne Ranelagh C.E. School. The original school building is now called Cranbourne Hall.

When the Grammar School at Bracknell was opened in 1908 it was named Ranelagh School. Cranbourne School then dropped the name Ranelagh but retained part of Lord Ranelagh's coat of arms on its badge. Today it is known as Cranbourne Primary School and caters for children of infant and junior age.

Lovel Road takes its name from the family who were important landowners in Norman times. Plaistow Green Farm, built in 1569, said to be originally a hunting lodge, has associations with the Jacobite Trust. An inscription on one of the walls reads:

C
1569   O U M D   ✳   1716
1 E

The six-pointed star is a Jacobite emblem. C 1 E refers possibly to the old Pretender, James Edward Stuart.

The winter quarters of Billy Smart's Circus are at St. George's stables in North Street. In the forecourt is a life-size bronze statue by Edwin Russell of the late Billy Smart, in a characteristic pose with his pet dog. They continue to put on three shows per year here, one of which is the Christmas Television show.

Crowthorne

The village of Crowthorne owes its existence to the proximity of Wellington College and Broadmoor Hospital, round which the village has grown. Wellington College, built about 1859, is a national memorial to the Duke of Wellington, whose name and those of his generals find echoes in the titles of roads and inns of the neighbourhood, e.g. Duke's Ride and the Iron Duke.

Broadmoor Hospital was built about the same time on a high spur of the ground near Caesar's Camp. According to an old resident, the former inhabitants of the district were known as Broom Squires or Broom Dashers, whom he described at "good-living people, having a semi-underground life, all of whom had an altar of sods with bits of glass stuck in the top". Such were the "Aborigines" of Crowthorne.

The Devil's Highway, a Roman road, crosses the village and two Roman milestones are in existence still. Although most buildings are modern, one Tudor cottage remains in the woods towards Owlsmoor. Crowthorne would appear to have wider boundaries than is expected, being bounded on one side by Owlsmoor, formerly called Newfoundland after an original squatter called New with numerous progeny; and on the other by California.

Crowthorne, once part of the Parish of Sandhurst, acquired its name because the postal authorities wished to give it a name to facilitate deliveries from Wokingham, instead of York Town, Surrey (which with Cambridge Town became known as Camberley). "Albertonville" had been suggested in honour of the Prince Consort, but luckily the suggestion of "Crowthorne", after some thorn trees at Brookers Corner, at the top of the village, was adopted. In Domesday Book, Crowthorne Farm appears as a seperate holding in the Royal Forest of Windsor, although the present farm holdings do not date back to the days of William the Conqueror.

Three men who died in the Crimean War at the famous Charge of the Light Brigade are buried in the old churchyard.

Since 1950, the population of Crowthorne has greatly increased, due partly to the setting up of the Road Research Laboratory and also to the building of quite a number of very attractive housing estates, otherwise the village is unchanged.

Cumnor The attractive stone-built village was formerly just within the northern boundary of Berkshire—the great city of Oxford is just over the border. William de Cumnor, 14th-century Abbot of Abingdon, gave his name to the village; but the person whose name is forever linked with this old place is the ill-fated Amy Robsart, first wife of Robert Dudley, Earl of Leicester, favourite of Elizabeth I. While the great gentleman peacocked at Court, Amy Robsart lived quietly at Cumnor Place until the day when all England learned that she had been found with a broken neck at the foot of her staircase. Did she fall, or was she pushed? This is one of the great unsolved historical mysteries.

Cumnor Place was demolished 200 years ago, but some of the windows are preserved in Wytham Church, and a staircase is still in a local farmhouse.

The greater part of the village, though very picturesque, dates mainly from 1930; but there are still a few old thatched cottages round the Church of St. Michael which contains some treasures worth seeing. There is a Jacobean reading desk, a chained Bible of 1611, a chancel brass to the last Abbot of Abingdon, a life-sized statue of Elizabeth I brought from the gardens of Cumnor Hall, and a number of letters from Amy Robsart to her husband and others kept in the vestry.

There is also in the Tower a splendid oak spiral staircase built round a huge oak pillar dated 1685.

The Warwick Coat of Arms, the Bear and Ragged Staff are preserved in the name of the ancient inn that was probably a farm-house of Cumnor Place in Tudor times. It has immensely thick buttressed stone walls, and some fine wood carvings above the windows.

Cumnor, old and new, has the mellow charm of a Cotswold stone village, and is well worth a visit.

Curridge The spelling of this village name has varied over the years, from Cusa's Ridge, Coseridge, to Custeridge . . . in A.D. 953 King Edred by a charter witnessed by a Bishop of Ramsbury gifted Custeridge to his thane, Alfwold.

King John is reported to have visited the little settlement in 1207 on his way to Woodstock, and Oliver Cromwell spent a night at the oldest house in Curridge, Lindley Farm.

Until the late 1960's the village was in the ecclesiastical parish of Chieveley, but it is now transferred to nearby Hermitage. The 19th-century church, which was merely one end of the church school-building, consisting of an apse with stained glass windows, has now been closed.

The old village centres round the Green, where Curridge Farm, a fine domestic building of late 16th or early 17th-century style, is situated. At Woodside Farm, during restorations, a child's leather lace-up boot, perfectly preserved, was discovered in the roof space, where such things were traditionally built in for luck.

The old village green has now been enclosed, but has served in the past as a site for nonconformist church meetings, village assemblies, and as a pound for cattle being driven to Newbury market.

Bricks and tiles used to be made at Curridge, but the claypits are now closed.

The famous cartoonist Mr. H. M. Bateman used to live in Curridge, and another celebrity of the fashion world, Mr. Jo Mattli, has a weekend cottage on the outskirts of the village.

The nearby intersection point on the M4 has brought this quiet little place within quick motoring distance of London. Its shopping centre is the market town of Newbury, only a few miles away.

The village hall was built and is still maintained by the W.I., and is beautifully set among trees and woodlands. There are many bridle-paths and rights-of-way in this delightful part of Berkshire, and being on white belt area protects it from any large scale development.

Drayton

The motorist speeding along the A34 towards Abingdon will pass two long lines of small bungalows in ribbon development, a few shops, and some fine old pink chestnut trees on a small green, and say to himself, that's Drayton!

If you turn off to the right at the green you will find the old village, mellow and leafy, with a wide High Street, green verges, some splendid chestnut trees and a number of beautiful old cottages.

Not quite so many as there used to be . . . Drayton, like many other little settlements, had its "great fire" in the days before piped water and fire brigades. On April 16th, 1780, the fire was described as "sweeping down the High Street", and many of the old thatched dwellings went in the blaze. Drayton picked itself up, raised the considerable sum of £3,066 5s. 9½d, and paid those who had suffered 15 per cent of their loss. They also built five almshouses at a cost of £283 18s. 9d. . . . you can still see the almshouses today.

The village has always been famous for its walnut trees, and though some landlords have cut them down for valuable timber, there are still quite a large number scattered through the various gardens.

Drayton Manor is an attractive house, not very large, mainly Tudor behind an 18th-century façade. It has passed through many hands, and was for a time in the possession of the Eyston family of East Hendred. A small Roman Catholic chapel attached to the house was destroyed in the Civil War.

The church is well worth a visit. It is small, basically 13th and 15th century, and much altered by enthusiastic Victorians in the 19th century; but it is beautifully kept and has great charm. A beautiful alabaster Reredos, now in the Lady Chapel, was partly stored in a vault in the church and discovered in 1814. There are several of similar design in Northamptonshire and one at Yarnton in Oxfordshire; informed opinion describes them as French in origin.

Abingdon provided Drayton with a curate for the church until 1868, when the first Vicar was appointed. A famous 18th-century churchman, Parson Woodforde, who wrote the well-known diaries descriptive of country life, is known to have preached at Drayton.

There is still a blacksmith in the village, but he is more concerned with wrought iron and repairing iron implements than with shoeing horses.

Until fairly recent years the Drayton Mummers performed their play and school children celebrated May Day with songs, dances and garlands of flowers.

From a much more ancient past comes a Bronze Age beaker, some Romano-British pottery, a Roman skeleton and many Saxon burial remains found in the old gravel pits.

Like many another old village, Drayton has its modern housing estates, which seem to be concentrated on the west side of the A34, while the old settlement lies to the east. Both of the local public houses are on the west side, the fast motor road having effectively split the village in two. The new A34, which passes west of the village, has thankfully taken much of the heavy traffic away and restored some of its former tranquility to this delightful small place.

Earley derives from Anglo-Saxon, Earn—eagle, and leah—a wood—eagle wood.

Domesday mentions two main manors—Erlegh St. Bartholomew, later known as Erlegh Court, and Erlegh St. Nicholas, later Erlegh White Knights—so named because of chapels dedicated to these two Saints on the two manors. Neither had font nor bell, but a wooden cross erected in an enclosed space on which palms were hung on Palm Sunday.

The de Erleghs held the manors for some centuries, one John de Erlegh in 1292 was known as "The White Knight"—hence the re-naming of the manor. The leper hospital of Reading Abbey owned lands at Earley White Knights, the revenue of which were devoted to lepers.

Earley nowadays is not a village in the true sense of the word, it is an extended area of Reading with its boundary only two miles from the busy town centre. It covers an area of approximately 2,000 acres and has a population of about 13,000, and has lost all traces of its ancient history.

The industry comprises a power station, one large, and several small factories. To the south there is development on a large scale, reducing the area of open farm land.

The old Dreadnought public house, once the only one in Earley, is used as a Sailing Club House by the University of Reading, who have also built a large Hall of Residence in Lower Earley.

The Parish Church of St. Peter was completed in 1844. At this time, looking towards Wokingham, Hungerford Lodge could be seen and one or two cottages where Earley Station now stands, but for the rest it was open country. On the left was Bulmershe Court, standing in extensive grounds, which has now been demolished to allow for a College of Higher Education surrounded by large playing fields, thus preserving a fine open space.

On the right of the Wokingham Road was the Maiden Erlegh Estate, later occupied by the millionaire Sol. Joel, who improved the amenities of the area by giving and developing a piece of land as a sports ground to the rear of the church.

In the 17th century Erlegh Court belonged to Sir Owen Buckingham, M.P., who was killed in a duel at Stanlake Hurst by Richard Aldworth. Erlegh Court was later the home of Addington, the statesman and Prime Minister, afterwards created Viscount Sidmouth. He gave the site for Reading Hospital (now the Royal Berkshire Hospital) and Lady Sidmouth endowed it.

Many famous people have contributed to the history of Earley, but unfortunately no tangible evidence of them remains today.

55

EASTBURY

Eastbury

The Lambourn Valley village of Eastbury lies beside the little river which is fed from springs in the Fishpond. Several delightfully named bridges cross the Lambourn . . . Top Arch, Gumbledons Bridge, Church Bridge, Pigs Bridge and Bottom Arch.

The open, undulating lands all around Eastbury were once reserved exclusively for the Royal Chase, and as far back as King John there have been hunting boxes in the district.

The church is dedicated to St. James the Greater, and was built in 1851. Visitors will be interested in the fine memorial window engraved by Lawrence Whistler, to the memory of the poet Edward Thomas and his wife, and dedicated on October 16th, 1971. Their younger daughter, who taught for 17 years at Lambourn School, originated the idea for the window, and 700 people from all parts of the world contributed to make it a reality.

Eastbury Manor, the old Vicarage, the old Forge are buildings of interest; the oldest and possibly the most beautiful is the Pigeon House, once a Priory of the monks of Wallingford. It has a notably fine dovecot of brick and flint, dated 1620, well preserved, and with nesting holes for 999 pigeons, an essential table delicacy in the 17th century.

At the Prayer Cross of St. Antolina, opposite the church, itinerant preachers, trade union agents and anyone with a speech to deliver, were able to shout their message to the passers-by.

In the 19th century it was a lively centre for heckling and demonstrations. In the 16th century religious processions took place from this Prayer Cross to the Wodebury Cross at Shefford Woodlands.

Street lighting came to Eastbury as early as 1897, and a plaque on one of the houses proudly announces this benefit to the old village.

East Garston
lies in a dip in the surrounding chalk downs of the Lambourn Valley. The name has varied considerably over the centuries, and was pronounced locally as Argasson until it settled down into its modern form.

The valley is known for its horses, and before the Norman Conquest, Esgar, Staller or Master of the Horses to Edward the Confessor, owned the Manor.

All Saints Church, cruciform in shape and built of flint and stone, has Norman features . . . a carved south doorway in the solid 16th-century porch, the blocked north door, and the fine pillar piscina. Before the Reformation it was rich in furniture, ornaments and vestments, but subsequently became so neglected that there was a complete restoration in 1876–82.

Goldhill House was mentioned as far back as 1469, and was originally a farmhouse within the Manor grounds, and was granted to John Estbury of Lambourn.

The 18th-century Manor House has a beautiful old tiled roof arranged in attractive patterns.

Isaac Early, a native of East Garston, died in 1912 at the age of 104, having been christened just before his second birthday. According to Church baptismal records, the Vicar, who must have been inordinately devoted to accuracy, could not decide whether the old man was 104 or 105, and allowed no tombstone on his grave.

Isaac Early was for 82 years a local preacher at the Primitive Methodist Chapel, and the foundations of the present chapel, built in 1860, contained stones collected by him and loaded into a wheelbarrow, which was pulled with a rope by his wife!

Excavations in 1923 verified that strip terrace cultivation at Westfields was done by ploughing in the 15th century.

In 1898 the railway came to the Lambourn Valley and East Garston, a single-line track. Alas, the village station has gone the way of many another in this age of progress.

Emmer Green

The name of the village is believed to be derived from an old Saxon word "Eamere", meaning "a lake beside a stream". The once sizeable lake is now but a pond; the stream could be "the Swillies", which runs from the west side of the pond down to the River Thames.

Cattle and horses of the local farmers came to drink from the one-time unfenced pond, and the carriers drove their horses through it to refresh them on long and tiring journeys.

Before piped water came to Emmer Green at the turn of the century, villagers relied upon the springs for their drinking water. One of these, Chalybete Spring in Surley Row, was reputed to have healing powers, especially for the eyes, and the water was regularly bottled and sold.

Villagers drew water from the pump opposite the pond, and carried it home with the aid of the yoke.

A stone dragon over Hodges Post-Office Stores was originally over the blacksmith's shop on that site, and was made at Emmer Green brickworks.

The blacksmith's shop, in an ideal position for travellers to and from Reading, probably dated back to the 16th century, and undoubtedly was one of the busiest spots in the area before the advent of the motor age.

The early 16th century White Horse Inn has Elizabethan oak beams and floor-boards. Until the 1920's groceries were sold over the counter and beer drawn from the barrel; skittles and quoits were the regular pastime of the locals there of an evening, right up to the end of World War I.

In the late 1800's and early this century, firemen had their headquarters in the yard of the early 19th-century Blackhorse Inn. Several residents still remember the firecart being pulled out by hand and, with much shouting and encouragement from the onlookers, charging off down the road.

In 1826 a Mrs. Burchett, who owned several farms in the area, was anxious for a chapel to be built on her land at Emmer Green. A Mr. Sherman accepted her offer, and in nine months' time the chapel was built with a tower of Bath stone. The graveyard was reputed to be the smallest in England with only one grave, that of a former minister.

What was once the open village green has now been fenced in as the village recreation ground, well maintained by Reading Corporation.

One event on the village green that assuredly caused great excitement was the building of a huge bonfire to celebrate the coronation of Edward VII. The bonfire was built up on a scaffold base, and was guarded by two men who sat inside the structure ready to deter any would-be fireraisers before time.

Within living memory, it was the custom at a funeral for six pall-bearers to carry the coffin on their shoulders from Emmer Green all the way to St. Peter's Church, Caversham, with a change of pall-bearers half-way. Old survey maps show a right of way from the pond, across fields to Bottle Cottage in Surley Row, then down Rotherfield Way.

Largely an agricultural area, a brick-kiln was built about 1654 on land known as Homer's Field, then under Sonning Manor. Water for a laundry owned by a Miss Fewster used to be fetched from the River Thames by cart twice daily.

Brickwall Cottages were originally the office and stables for the horses used on the brickfield.

During the last war the Reading archives were stored in underground caves in the area, as were cardboard coffins ready for possible gas victims—praise be they never needed to be used! The caves are very large, extending from the old brick-kiln, under Kiln Road, and beneath woods on the other side. They came into being when chalk was quarried for agricultural purposes.

Rosehill House, standing in 14 acres of grounds, was once part of Caversham Manor, the first building being erected in 1791. Martin John Sutton lived there, the house then being called Kidmore Grange. In 1923 it was bought for the Oratory Prep. School, then from the outbreak of the last war until 1958 it served as Salvation Army H.Q. The house is now converted into flats and the grounds make up a fine housing estate.

The first village school was built in 1866, but demolished ten years later when a new one was erected. This in turn was closed in 1933 through lack of support. In September 1950 the first modern primary school opened in Peppard Road, followed by another in Grove Road, and a year later a secondary school was started at The Grove.

The foundation stone of St. Barnabas Church was laid in 1924, and the Church was consecrated five years later.

St. Benet's Home, built and maintained by Dr. Powell of Derby Road in 1902, is now a Church of England Home for young boys who attend the local school.

There are a number of springs (now underground) in the area, and over the years swallow holes have appeared. In 1955 people noticed an unpleasant smell at a pond in Camp Wood—then with a loud noise the pond suddenly soaked away! But that was not all

59

—three hours later, with an explosive roar, four fully-grown trees disappeared into the ground in a matter of seconds, setting up a great water spout.

Sixty-five years before, near Brickwall House, locals enjoyed themselves at one of the regular dances held in a small hall, then made their way home, unaware how near they were to tragedy. By next morning the hall had been swallowed up into the ground!

The garden of 164 Kidmore End Road appears to be a virtual treasure trove, having yielded, amongst other things, a 150,000,000-year-old Coxcomb Oyster, prehistoric hand axes, Roman and 16th century coins and medieval pottery.

Surley Row is a very ancient, narrow, winding road, around which are a number of interesting houses, including Caversham Hill, c. 1810, the Tudor Old Grove House, and No. 46 Surley Row, which used to be the 18th-century Gardeners' Arms.

Hightown Secondary School now occupies the Queen Anne mansion, Caversham Grove. How many of the children who crowd the "assembly hall" realize, one wonders, that they are in a 16th-century tithe barn?

Enborne & Hamstead Marshall

These two small villages lie close together and are bordered by the River Kennet and the Enborne. Like most of Berkshire, this is historic ground, the first battle of Newbury having been fought near Enborne Heath, where a 15-lb. cannon ball was found only a few years ago.

The great park of Hamstead Marshall was originally the home of the Earls Marshall, and is mentioned in Domesday Book. The big house today, owned by Lord Craven, has been made into a nursing home.

The church of St. Michael and All Angels stands among farm buildings on land once owned by Romsey Abbey, and the interior bears some resemblance to the Abbey. The Norman nave, a fine wall painting, and an early font with emblems of the Passion, are all of interest. A very ancient bell is known as the Michael bell.

In Hamstead Park the church is dedicated to St. Mary, and has an early English chancel arch and traces of a rood screen, but the tower, pulpit, gallery and panelling are Jacobean.

The Craven Hounds meet in the park, and there is an annual Horse Show and Fête.

The post office was unfortunately closed in recent years. There are two hotels which serve meals, one claiming to be the oldest in Berkshire.

Englefield six miles west of Reading, commemorates a battle fought between the Saxons and the Danes in A.D. 871 — "open land of the Angles". The *Anglo-Saxon Chronicle* states that: "In this year came the host to Reading in Wessex, and three days afterwards two jarls rode up-country; then ealdorman Aethelwulf opposed them at Englefield and fought against them and won the victory. Four days afterwards King Aethelred and Alfred, his brother, led great levies there to Reading, and fought against the host; and great slaughter was made there on either side, and ealdorman Aethelwulf was slain, and the Danes had possession of the place of slaughter."

Englefield is a small village, privately owned by the squire, Mr. William Benyon, M.P., with outlying villages included.

Englefield House, built probably in the mid-16th century, was severely damaged by fire in 1886, and had to be largely rebuilt from the design of the London architect Richard Armstrong. Nevertheless, it has not changed much since Dance painted it in the late 18th century, and Constable in 1832, except that the front door has been closed up, and Victorian pinnacles stand against the sky.

The principal rooms of the house are large and Victorian, notably the hall under the tower, running up through two storeys and open to a wide gallery or corridor on the ground as well as the first floor. Their decoration was not included in Armstrong's bill of 1886, which amounted to £2,556 17s.

The mansion has been occupied by many men of note: Sir Francis Englefield, more than likely the original owner, was a Catholic, so wisely absented himself from England between 1559 and 1589; in which year it passed to the Earl of Essex, executed in 1601. The Marquis of Winchester then moved in, and after him Sir Francis Walsingham, Secretary of State to Queen Elizabeth. In 1573, he played an important part in the discovery of the Babington Plot, aimed at the assassination of the Queen and the placing of Mary Queen of Scots on the throne.

Elizabeth I and II, as well as many other members of the Royal Family, have been frequent visitors to the house.

The ghost of another owner, Powlett Wright, Esq., is reputed to haunt the house and the tunnel (now blocked up) under the back region of the building. Many bygone villagers have reputedly given evidence to this effect, and with a house so steeped in history it is small wonder, perhaps, that it should still be visited in spiritual form, by one or other of its colourful owners.

Until more recent years, a Harvest Home was celebrated with

a service in St. Mark's Church, where in older times was St. Mary's Chantry, attended by all employees and their families. This was followed by a dinner for the men in the Long Gallery of Englefield House, and then sports and entertainment in the park and a sumptuous tea for the women and children. Included amongst the usual church festivals is an annual Nativity Play performed by local schoolchildren.

The original village school has now been modernized, and a number of the older cottages remain, while the lodges were built in 1862.

A very fine social club, cricket ground with pavilion, and football ground, privately owned estate works, and village stores contribute towards the self-sufficiency of the village, while all the male population are employed on the Englefield Estate, in either agricultural, gardening or maintenance capacities.

The population has declined during the last 110 years, some estate cottages having been demolished. The number of schoolchildren during the late 1890's and early 1900's was over 150, while the entire population now is approximately 220.

Some of the place-names of the village speak vividly of bygone customs—did Deadman's Lane once lead to a gibbet? Imagine the stately traffic bowling down Coach Road, or the stray cattle and sheep being herded into the Pound after being found wandering down Common Hill.

Englefield House is open to the public every spring, as are the very fine gardens, and various shows in the park include pony jumping, cricket matches, and Rolls-Royce car rallies—a far cry from the hawking and hunting for the privileged few in the time of the first lords of the manor of Englefield.

Fernham This little hamlet of 180 souls, near to Faringdon, has remained much the same size for as long as its oldest inhabitants can remember. The thatched cottages and more modern houses cluster round a small green by the post office and bakery, and others centre on the Woodman, an old village inn.

The church of St. John the Divine was built in 1860 by the Reverend John Hughes, and is a chapel-of-ease, shared with the village of Longcot. The little Victorian "dame school" next to the church once taught the Fernham children for one penny a week.

Everything in Fernham is simple and basic—Chapel Lane leads to the disused Congregational Chapel, now a youth club and village hall. Church Lane is a cul-de-sac, with a footpath leading to the

Manor Farm, comfortably called the Milk Path for obvious reasons.

There is a village pump on the Green, timbered and roofed over, no longer in use, but charming and picturesque, and the sole source of water in Fernham only fifty years ago.

The post office and bakery is an old and delightful building, Fernham Manor stands on the road to Faringdon, and the original Ringdale Manor is now St. Mary's Priory, a Roman Catholic community of the Benedictine Order, where the Nuns have a nursery school. Further up the hill is the new Ringdale Manor, home of Sir John Walker.

The quiet village of Fernham has suffered from twentieth-century progress—the railway has been closed and the bridge demolished, so the heavy traffic between Oxford and Swindon has taken to the road; the great juggernauts of transport are bringing noise, dirt and danger to yet another green and pleasant corner of our county.

Finchampstead is blessed with distinct traces of its early history—part of the Roman Road from London to Bath, via Silchester (Calleva Atrebatum), running right through the parish, marked on the map as the Devil's Highway.

Entering the parish as Roman Ride, it may still be traced past the Queen's Oak, to the left of White Horse Lane, through Webb's Farm fields, on to West Court built on the road itself, then across Arborfield Road. In 1841 a Roman milestone was discovered in Six Acres field and removed to the garden of Bannisters.

Elevated ground surrounding the church point to it probably having been a fortified Roman camp.

Some walls and the very fine font of St. James's Church are the original, possibly Norman. The extremely interesting piscina and credence are probably unique, and the semi-circular apse is a rare feature in English churches, most having been squared off in later construction.

An oak tree facing the churchyard entrance was planted on June 21st, 1887, commemorating Queen Victoria's Golden Jubilee.

The original manor probably stood on Church Hill, divided, about 1290, into the east and west moieties of the Manor of Finchampstead. Sir William Banastre left the manor and advowson of the church between his two daughters, East and West Courts becoming their respective homes.

A certain Banastre apparently betrayed Sir Henry Stafford, Duke of Buckingham, to his death in 1483. The present house, Banisters, was built in Charles II's reign on the site of an older property.

The Manor of Finchamestede Mill, in Domesday Book, yielded to the King 7s. 6d. The well-preserved, very old "Thatched Cottage", now the village shop, was once the smithy, reputedly haunted. An active thatcher still lives in the village.

In 1858 Mr. John Walter of Bearwood, owner of East Court for 45 years, provided the first school buildings. In 1971 Mr. W. R. van Straubenzee, M.B.E., M.P., opened the latest extension, paid for in part by people of the parish.

John Walter was also responsible for the Sequoia Pine-lined road over the Ridges to Wellington College Station, opened to the public in 1863.

The Ridges, National Trust property since 1913, command a view over the Blackwater Valley to Hindhead, south-west to Cottingham Clump, and west to Inkpen Beacon, now somewhat obscured by tree growth.

To these Ridges Henry VII is said to have ridden, with Prince Arthur, to meet Katherine of Aragon after her arrival in England, as the Prince's bride. Spanish custom forbade a bride to be seen by the groom till after the marriage ceremony, but Katharine lifted her veil to face Arthur. We can picture the stately procession, next day, to Chertsey; little did that young Spanish girl know what lay ahead of her during her eventful and tragic stay in England!

King Oswald of Northumbria was closely concerned, in 634 A.D., with Bishop Birinus in bringing Christianity to this part of the country. In 635 he stood sponsor for King Cyneglis, King of Wessex, when he was converted by Bishop Birinus. Dozell's well, on Fleet Hill, in the 10th and 11th centuries, was said to have possessed marvellous curative properties, especially for eye diseases. It was described in the *Saxon Chronicle* as "boiling up with streams of blood, whose waters made red all others where they came, to the great amazement of the beholders. . ." This occurrence was regarded as a sign of impending national calamity. The well was accidentally destroyed in 1872, by deepening of the ditch, but there is still a constant trickle of water on the spot. An adjacent property has recently been re-named "Constant Spring".

Today visitors flock to the Ridges, and to Lady Liddell's beautiful garden at White Horse (originally the stables of the Manor by the church), open to the public in aid of charities. Heath Pool is another unspoilt attraction.

Off the Nine Mile Ride which was built by soldiers disbanded after the Jacobite Rebellion, is the new well-planned Gorse Rise Housing Estate.

The social centre of the village is the fine Memorial Hall built in 1960, with sporting activities taking place in the Park.

The annual fête is a popular meeting-place for the world and his wife, when the spirit of the village is truly in evidence.

Greenham

About two miles east of Newbury, and between the Kennet and Enborne Rivers, the parish of Greenham extends over beautifully wooded common land. Some delightful houses, both old and new, are tucked in among the trees, and Greenham has several historic claims to fame.

A hospice of the Order of St. John once stood here, and Newbury Castle controlled the important river crossing over the River Kennet. Downstream at Greenham Mills, to win a wager of 1,000 guineas, a sheep was shorn at daybreak, the wool spun, woven into cloth, and made into a coat in 13 hours 20 minutes.

There is a fine Jesse window in the parish church of St. Mary, built in 1875 by Woodyer to replace a much older partly wooden structure. The window glass is Flemish and dates from 1618.

Sandleford Priory, near the Winchester Road and now a private school for girls, was originally a monastry founded in the 12th century for the Augustinian Canons. The Prior, Simon Dana, was deposed in 1440 for allowing the house to become ruinous and for "other faults" which can only be guessed at.

In the 18th century the Priory became the home of the Montague family, and that original blue-stocking, Lady Montague, here entertained the literary lions of the day . . . Samuel Johnson, Oliver Goldsmith, Dr. Stilling Fleet and others.

Greenham Lodge, formerly the home of the Lord of the Manor, Mr. L. H. Baxendale, was built in 1875 after the style of Shaw House. This same squire with a Mr. Porter built the Newbury Racecourse, which lies within Greenham parish.

The racecourse has been variously used since its completion . . . it was a P.o.W. camp in the 1914–18 War, and an American Army supply depot in the last war.

Greenham Airfield was constructed in 1940 to accommodate U.S. Air Force gliders, and rebuilt in 1954 for the use of N.A.T.O. aircraft. Now it is retained as an emergency base and for occasional flying exercises.

Since 1970 three housing developments have taken place, which includes a Community Centre, and the population is now approximately 1,800.

The Hagbournes

If you want to see a beautiful old village, walk along the main road of East Hagbourne from Lower Cross to St. Andrew's Church . . . about half a winding mile of visual delight. The old cottages and houses, black and white thatched, mellow red Georgian, a few Victorian, are individually interesting; but it is the overall grouping, the lovely line of roofs and gables that most pleases a discerning eye.

The earliest clue to the name HAGBOURNE is in a charter of King Alfred, which speaks of HACCA BURN or HACCA BROC. Hacca was probably a Saxon chief, and certainly his brook is still there . . . it flows around the moated Manor House, through a number of residents' gardens, before it finally goes underground.

From Domesday Book we know that East Hagbourne belonged to Rainbald, a Norman priest who founded the Abbey of Cirencester, and was Chancellor to Edward the Confessor.

It is probable that the church today grew from the 11th-century Saxon church, with additions through the centuries—the nave and chancel were built in the 12th century on an earlier foundation. You will find St. Andrew's Church well worth visiting . . . it has a Sanctus bell-cote on the square tower, a Sanctuary Knocker on the door, some good memorial brasses, and a noble peal of eight bells. A bell still in use was donated by Alice Aldworth of West Hagbourne, at a cost of sixteen pence, in 1545.

The Great Fire of Hagbourne in 1659 destroyed the cottages that stretched across the fields beside the brook to West Hagbourne, and now the two villages are quite separate. A proclamation of Charles II, dated 1661, drew attention to "the great impoverishment and deplorable conditions of the poor inhabitants of our town of East Hagbourne", and Londoners collected money for their relief. In 1666 the Great Fire of London inspired the villagers of the Hagbournes to return their charity, and money was sent for the relief of London!

Three Medieval Crosses once stood in East Hagbourne, but today only one remains—the lovely Upper Cross near the church, with five steps and two sundials on the top. Two broken stumps are all that remain of the Lower Cross and the Coscote Cross.

Owing to an apprentice's mistake, blotting paper was invented in East Hagbourne; when the astute paper makers realised its commercial value, the trade grew too large for the little village, and the paper mill moved to Essex.

East Hagbourne has three inns, all with a friendly, club atmosphere . . . the Fleur de Lys, on Main Road, the Traveller's Welcome at Lower Cross, and the Spread Eagle on Blewbury Road.

West Hagbourne

Walk across the fields by Church Path for three-quarters of a mile, or drive by the slightly longer road via Coscote, and you come to West Hagbourne. Once joined to its sister village, it is now a hamlet on its own, with no shop, church, school or village hall, but sharing these amenities with East Hagbourne. It has, however, its own inn, the Horse and Harrow. About three hundred souls live here, in a central core of old cottages, farmhouses and new bungalows along the main road, with a fringe of Council estates on the edges. A fine Georgian farmhouse Grove Manor Farm, sits just off the Church Path, and York Farm, Ivy Farm and the Manor Farm all have their houses in the village.

A handful of beautiful old cottages attracts photographers, and the main feature is the village pond, tree-shaded and lively with ducks and moor-hens. Any weekend you will find the odd car parked by the pond, and enthusiastic children feeding the very well nourished ducks.

West Hagbourne lies quarter of a mile off the A417 (Wantage to Reading road) and about 1¾ miles from Didcot.

Hare Hatch,
Kiln or Cutlers Green, Yeldall and part of Knowl Hill are all small hamlets which clustered on the edge of the Great Frith or Thicket, long before the road from London to Reading had any significance. They are in the parish of Wargrave.

Hare Hatch is noted for its many smaller but attractive estates that stand back from the coaching road, and which centre round the Horse and Groom, an old hostelry on the main Bath Road. The oldest family is the Youngs, who came to Hare Hatch in the early 17th century. The seat known as the "Rest and be thankful" (this instruction is carved on the seat) was donated by one of the family in the mid-19th century, and kept in good repair by them until taken over by the Wokingham District Council.

In the 18th century Richard Edgeworth and his family came to dwell at Hare Hatch. He made a runaway match with a girl of 15 whom he married at Gretna Green. (It was his only unhappy marriage. He had four wives altogether and 19 children.) Edgeworth brought his eldest son and his daughter Maria from Oxford when he moved to Hare Hatch. Here they found themselves neighbours of Thomas Day, the author of *Sandford and Merton*. Day had the odd notion of bringing up two foundling girls, one of whom he intended to make his wife when old enough, but it was Edgeworth who married the prettiest. Maria's gift as a story-teller was early recognised by her father and he encouraged her to write not only novels but serious books on education.

Harwell
Set among farmlands and orchards on the ancient Portway, equally between Wallingford and Wantage, is the old village of Harwell. It is a district of wells and springs, and in Saxon days was known as Hares Well, later becoming Harewell. A medieval John de Harewell, King's Clerk, became the Bishop of Bath and Wells.

Ulfric, a Saxon Freeman, held the Manor of Harwell in the reign of Edward the Confessor; with the Norman Conquest it passed into the hands of Roger d'Ivry, and there are records of a chapel here in 1086. From the 12th to the 14th centuries there were additions and alterations, and the fine church of St. Matthew stands today a monument to centuries of loving craftsmanship.

The people of Harwell have always been practical; and until the old church gallery which housed the choir and organ was dismantled, they kept the village fire-engine and buckets under the gallery. A disastrous fire in 1852 swept through the High Street, and nine farms, twenty-three cottages, livestock, hay and straw were destroyed. Victorian houses were built to replace the ancient thatched cottages, but there are still fine examples of the earliest Cruck cottages in Harwell . . . Dell Cottage, Le Carillon, School House and Pomander House are all worth looking at.

Notable houses to look for are Prince's Manor, with 17th-century features, and much earlier 14th-century fabric. The Prince in the name was the Black Prince, who gave the manor to the College of St. Nicholas, Wallingford. Richard Loder bought it back in 1557, and the Loder family records show sales of the famous Harwell cherries at Abingdon market from 1610 to 1620. John Lay bought Prince's Manor from the Loders in 1840 and members of the Lay family are still living there.

Middle Farm, which is also called Bayliol's or Bronz's Manor, is a beautiful house in the High Street. Parts of this house are 13th century, and although the great central hall has been divided into two floors, much of the interior is essentially unchanged since 1590.

Wellshead Farm, to the south of the church, partly 14th century and partly 16th century, is a charming house with a stream running through the garden. It had a long period of being divided into two, but is now happily restored to its earlier state.

Harwell's most infamous historical character was Piers Gaveston. He was given the Manor of Harwell by his devoted Edward II, who also lavished on him much of the Queen's dowry and all her jewels. Gaveston Way preserves the favourite's name in Harwell, and his Coat of Arms adorns the east window of St. Matthew's Church.

Harwell's population is now over 2,220, with several new housing estates and a fine modern Infant and Junior School. It has a great many community associations and interests, including a lively Women's Institute of over 100 members. It is a good place to live in and an attractive place to visit.

Hatford

The village of Hatford lies about three and a half miles south-east of Faringdon, an ancient and historic little market town.

Hatford has a pleasant situation, and lies almost within the valley of the White Horse. It covers approximately 950 acres.

On entering the village from Faringdon, Hatford Manor House is predominant, with the old church of St. George close by. The origin of the Manor is somewhat obscure, but we know it was there at the time of the Domesday Survey. Many notable families have lived at the Manor, among them the Phellips, 1415. Alice Phellip, wife of Sir John Phellip, made three marriages, the third being to William de la Pole, Duke of Suffolk, by whom she had a son, and from this line descended the Duke of Suffolk who was executed for treason.

Thus Hatford Manor, and all estate annexed, was forfeited to the Crown. The Manor was then granted to Cecily, wife of Sir Alexander Unton; their son Edward—afterwards Sir Edward— married Anne, Countess of Warwick, daughter of the Protector Somerset.

The 18th century saw the manor much altered.

Deeply interesting is the old church of St. George, situated between Hatford Manor and what was the Rectory (dated 1869). The church was originally Norman, and possessed a small tower. It still retains many beautiful features. The south door is a good example of Norman work, as is the Chancel arch and another plain door and window.

Owing to the church of St. George lapsing into a state of serious decay, a new church was built during the years 1873–74 and dedicated to The Holy Trinity. The outer skin of this church is a fine example of random coursed stonework. Sad to relate, The Holy Trinity was declared redundant early this year (1972) and was recently put up for sale!

Thus St. George's has now turned full circle, its Chancel roof has been repaired and it serves the village again for divine worship.

Over the years the size of the village has changed little, its maximum population never seems to have been more than 120 people. It sports no village pub, no shops, and, alas, no bus service. It must have been a strange quirk of fate when the Germans singled the village out for a high explosive bomb during the 1939– 45 war. Traces of this disaster have now long since vanished, and with it the village pub.

The school room, though still standing, no longer serves the village children, but is used as a meeting-place for Faringdon Young Farmers.

EAST HENDRED

East Hendred

The traveller in search of a perfect old Downland village need go no further than East Hendred. It lies off the main road between Abingdon and the West, surrounded by fields and orchards, and behind it the North Berkshire Downs. Go on foot if you can, for the little winding lanes, tight-packed with old cottages and crooked pavements, go round about like a small labyrinth to which one has lost the guiding thread. Cruck Cottages, Tudor brick, Georgian plaster, cheek by jowl . . . lovely at any time in the year. But walk the quiet roads on an evening of winter snow, and you will see, not a cosy Christmas card, but Medieval England.

Once a thriving wool town, Hendred had five manors . . . Abbey Manor, King's Manor, Framptons, the Manor of Arches, and one other belonging to New College, Oxford.

Today the Manor of Arches is called Hendred House, and turns a pale painted façade with tall Tudor chimneys to the world. Behind are Georgian and Victorian wings, and in the oldest part of the house the private chapel of St. Amand and St. John the Baptist. Pope Alexander IV gave his permission for the building of this chapel in 1256, and here the Catholic family of Eyston has lived and worshipped since the 14th century. No other service than the Roman Catholic has ever been heard in this church. This is seemly when one knows that the Eyston family are descendants of that great Catholic, Sir Thomas More, now a canonised saint of the Church he refused to renounce. His son, John More, married Anne Cresacre, the heiress of Barnborough, Yorkshire, and from them the last male descendant was the Jesuit Father Thomas

More, who died in 1795. His sister Bridget More married Peter Metcalfe; their son married Teresa Throckmorton, whose daughter, Maria Teresa, married Charles Eyston (1790–1857).

Hendred House has many family treasures, including Sir Thomas More's drinking cup, and the silver-banded ebony staff that supported Bishop Fisher on his way to the scaffold.

A copy of the famous painting of Sir Thomas More and his family (which hangs in the National Portrait Gallery) is to be seen in Hendred House. The beautiful parish church of St. Augustine sits on a slight rise in the centre of the village, and has a famous "faceless" clock, made by Seymons of Wantage in 1525, and still keeps good time. It is wound daily, and at three-hour intervals plays an old hymn tune, "The Angel's Hymn". A Burial Chantry, sometimes called the Eyston Chapel, remained the property of the Eyston family through all the religious persecutions, and is still a part of the Anglican Church.

The Roman Catholic Church of St. Mary was built and endowed by Charles John Eyston in 1865.

Old Hendred families seem to remain constant through the centuries . . . Castle, Roberts, Goddard, Day, Cowderey and Champ are but a few; the Cowdereys lent a wonderful collection of costumes, jewellery, old implements and documents to a recent village exhibition; and Champ's Chapel is still the name given to a wayside chapel of the Carthusian monks which enthusiasts plan to turn into a museum.

If you are in Hendred on Shrove Tuesday you will hear the children singing an old rhyme:

> Pit, pat, pan's hot,
> Here we come a' shroving,
> With the butcher up my back
> A ha'penny's better than nothing!

For this they each are given a current bun and a half-penny by the squire, Mr. Thomas More Eyston.

On the Day of St. Thomas the Apostle, flour is distributed to widows and widowers of the parish.

A building of special interest is Mr. Wicken's shop, a beautiful piece of herringbone brickwork and half-timbering.

Pause outside the handsomely restored Plough Inn, and you will find a plaque to puzzle the passer-by:

HERESTO PANDS PEN D ASOCI AL HOU R INHAR M (LES SMIRT) HA ND

FUNLET FRIENDS HIPRE I GN BE JUSTAN DK INDAN DEVIL EPEAKOF NO NE.

72

Hendred is a racing village with two training stables, and daily strings of beautiful horses can be seen exercising on the Downs. Wandering through the village goes a little road called Cat Street, but it has no feline associations; it is Hendred's abbreviation of St. Catherine's Street, and is somehow typical of the religious overtones of this ancient place.

East Hendred is a Conservation area and has been given a Village Plan . . . it need not fear a future urban sprawl.

Hermitage

There is a well still in existence in the grounds of Hermitage House which was once considered holy, and a cure for sore eyes; it is most likely that at one time a hermit cared for the well, and the name Hermitage stems from that time.

This is a beautiful village in undulating country with extensive woodlands; there are a number of old cottages but many more of Victorian date or more modern design.

The railway brought great changes to Hermitage in 1874, when a double track was built from Didcot to Newbury, with a local station and a halt at Pinewood for the brickfields. The "navigators" lived in huts and tents at Pinewood, and their riotous behaviour became a local scandal. To curb their drunkenness the Vicar, with help from the Methodists, built a coffee house to attract them, but with what success there is no record. Like other stations and railways, this line was closed in 1964, and the problem of what to do with the track is still unresolved.

The Church of Holy Trinity was built in 1835 by the Vicar of Hampstead Norreys, who was personal chaplain to Queen Adelaide, wife of William IV. Royalty contributed to the cost of the building and gave a set of Communion Plate. The attractive lych-gate was the gift of Colonel C. J. West in 1947, as a memorial to his wife.

The Church School, built in 1839 at a cost of £250 and an additional £260 in 1876, was bought by a public-spirited group of residents and converted to a fine Village Hall in 1962.

Within an Iron Age earthworks known as Grimsbury Castle or Devil's Bury, is a Folly called Grimsbury Tower, an octagonal brick structure with battlements and a pyramid roof. One of the upper rooms is said to be haunted, with an "ineradicable blood-stain" on the wall.

The M4 motorway passes near to Hermitage, with an intersection point only three miles away. It is possible that the coming

of the motorway may affect the village as much as the new railway did in Victorian days.

Close to the large village of Hermitage is the tiny hamlet of
Oare, the history of which goes back to A.D. 968 when King Edgar
gave Orha to the great Abbey of Abingdon.

Since the beginning of this century its quiet rural charm has
remained unchanged, but the last decade has altered its former
tranquillity. The constant rumble of traffic, day and night, on the
M4 motorway reminds one that the original peaceful atmosphere
has vanished completely.

Oare now consists of the Church of St. Bartholomew, pictur-
esquely situated and in regular use; a common, two farms, various private dwellings and cottages, with an estimated total population of 50 people.

Hinton Waldrist

This attractively named village
houses about 300 people and lies just
off the Faringdon to Oxford Road, A420. The setting is flat farmlands, the life is rural, and its history is long.

Hinton is the Saxon name for a village or homestead on high
ground, and Waldrist is a corruption of the name St. Valery, the
family who held the Manor in the 13th century.

Hinton Manor stands today on the site of an older house, but
the signs of a moat are still there. The owner in 1627 was the
regicide, Sir Henry Marten, who was one of the signatories of the
death warrant of Charles I; in fact, in 1655 the manor became the
property of the Lord Protector, Oliver Cromwell.

Local tradition has it that Cromwell and his men were quartered
for a time at Hinton Manor during the Civil War, and certainly
canonballs and weapons have been found in this much-fought-over
part of Berkshire.

The church, which probably dates from the 13th century, is
dedicated to St. Margaret of Antioch in Pisidia, a saint more
popular in the Middle Ages.

Hinton Waldrist was a great hunting village, and from 1658 the
Loder family lived at the Manor; one member, John Loder, was
a founder Member and Master of the Berkshire Hunt in the late
18th century.

In 1805 John Loder's son-in-law sold the hounds, and Hinton
Waldrist ceased to be the headquarters of the Old Berks. Hunt.

There are several attractive stone houses, including the Manor
and the Grange, both owned by the Davenport family, and a

number of lovely thatched cottages. On a stone in the Grange barn is painted the word JUBILEE, commemorating Queen Victoria's celebrations in 1887, when the village was entertained to dinner in the barn, and three beautiful Wellingtonias were planted at the entrance to the Manor.

The little hamlet of Duxford is part of the parish of Hinton Waldrist, and claims to be the ford over the River Dux that William the Conqueror chose to march his armies across after Hastings. Other Berkshire fords also claim this distinction. Duxford once had its own witch, and there are Victorian legends to prove it. She seems to have been an amicable witch, for her help was sought when the horses pulling a lady's hearse refused to budge, and she suggested two milk white martens would be better for the job. One feels that the Witch of Duxford kept her tongue firmly in her cheek.

Another claim to distinction is that in a land of inns and ale-houses Hinton Waldrist has never owned a public house. It has, however, a fine village hall given by Lady Page about 1921, and most local activities take place in this comfortable centre.

There is no longer a school in the parish and the children go by bus to the fine new school at neighbouring Longworth.

Hurley

The ancient village of Hurley is halfway between London and Oxford, being 55 miles from both by river. Although the name stems from the Saxon meaning "bend by the river" it has been occupied since the Bronze Age.

Domesday Book (A.D. 1086) records a church at Hurley, a manor with 25 villeins, 12 cottagers, 10 serfs, 19 ploughs, a mill, 2 fisheries, 20 acres of meadow, a wood for swine and about 120 acres of arable land. William the Conqueror removed the Saxon owner Esgar and conferred the property upon the Norman Baron Geoffrey de Mandeville. In 1976 the villagers bought this ancient lordship of the manor for £2,500. A wall plaque and a hand-inscribed book record the story and names of subscribers.

Some two miles from the village is the old mansion-house of Hall Place, now the Berkshire College of Agriculture. Hurley Farms Ltd., covering the land between the river and the main Henley–Maidenhead road, is owned and farmed by the Burfitt family, of whom three generations live in the village. Of the six pubs, the most interesting is the Dewdrop on Ashley Hill, founded for the use of the Windsor Forest foresters; and the Old Bell. The latter was built in 1187 as the guest-house of Hurley Priory. It has since risen in the social scale from a village inn to a world-famous hotel-restaurant owned and run by Mr. Trapani and his Italian staff. The Priory was founded by de Mandeville for a cell of monks from the Benedictine Abbey at Westminster in 1086, and endowed with the avowsons of many of the surrounding churches.

There are three noteworthy mansions in the village. Manor House and Ladye Place (both now divided into separate freeholds) and Hurley House. Hurley House is 17th century and probably built as a dower house to the original Ladye Place, down by the river. Ladye Place belonged to the Lovelaces but was pulled down in 1837, having failed to find a buyer. In its crypt, all that remains today, the 1688 "Glorious Revolution" was plotted by Lord John Lovelace, to place on the throne of England the Prince of Orange and his Stuart consort, as William III and Mary.

Adjacent to Hurley House, in the High Street, are three 17th-century almshouses, in the trusteeship of Hurley Church Estate, and one now serves as the village Post Office. In 1969 they were completely restored at a cost of £5,000. Church House next door dates from about 1490 and was built by the parishioners on ground gifted to them by the Prior of Hurley. For five centuries the rent was used to pay for the repairs to the church (often a cause for dispute). In 1971 Church House passed into private ownership, being sold for £10,125 to cover essential repairs required by the church. In 1975 the south end, called Church House Cottage, was also sold to the same buyer.

The remains of the Priory, dissolved by Henry VIII in 1536, centre round the church. The original Cloisters and monks' dormitories can be identified by the stone stringing and blocked-up windows and doors. The modern houses probably mark the original lay-out. The enormous Tithe Barn, converted into a private residence in 1950, and the unusually well preserved dovecote date from the mid-13th century, and show to some extent the wealth of the Priory.

A permanent settlement for 500 caravans and 30-odd caravan-type chalets built by Mr. Burfitt, is sited on the river bank. It is cheek by jowl to a very old cottage known as the Poisoned Duck. The name is thought to be derived from "Poisson Duc", the Norman-French for pike. The village boasts an active social life centred on the Church and Village Hall.

Hurley is a magnet for visitors at all seasons of the year with its open-air swimming facilities and ancient history. In winter, members of the London Angling Association arrive in five or six coaches in the grey dawn, to spend the whole day, like Jeremy Fisher, in the mud by the river, each under his huge green or black umbrella. In 1974 the village was honoured when Her Majesty the Queen walked to the Lock and boarded a river steamer to make her first trip on her own royal river down to Runnymede.

Hurst

". . . John of Hurst presented his chaplain, Richard by name, born at Ross . . . he is a youth and knoweth nothing . . ." Such was the unflattering report on the priest in charge of St. Nicholas's Church, Hurst, dependency of the Mother Church at Sonning on the Visitation of the Dean of Sarum in A.D. 1222.

This was the first Visitation of the Dean to Sonning and its dependent churches since the Synod of Oxford, in the same year, ordered that archdeacons ensure that ". . . priests can properly pronounce at least the words of the canon and baptism, and that they rightly understand this part. . . ." The majority of priests examined did not excel themselves, and Richard was not alone in his apparent complete ignorance of the Scriptures and, in many cases, complete inability to read the simplest sentence.

Hurst was an ancient parish even in the 13th century. The name means a "wood" in Old English and, before a clearing was made, the area was a thickly wooded part of the great Windsor Forest—there still exist two three-cornered pieces of land that separated bridle paths through the trees. The yew tree at the entrance to the church is said to be very old, perhaps the remaining representative of that great swathe of forest where wild boar and deer roamed at will. The settlement remained part of Windsor Forest until 1700, when it became a village in its own right.

St. Nicholas's Church was built in 1084, two years before the mammoth Domesday Book, in which the parish is named "Whistley", still represented by part of the parish called Whistley Green. The church was rebuilt in 1300, when the annual value of the living was £9 11s. 8d., and enlarged in 1520 . . . the year Henry VIII met Francis on the Field of the Cloth of Gold, chocolate was first introduced into Europe from Mexico, and Michelangelo built his famous Tomb Chapel of Medici in Florence. Although distinctly "Victorianized", the church still shows signs of its early building, has a simple Elizabethan pulpit from which Archbishop Laud preached on occasions, fine 17th-century plate and monuments, including one of a praying child and a distinctly frightening skeleton.

The fact that the church is separated from much of the village suggests that Hurst was a victim of the dreaded Black Death, more

77

than likely in 1348, the year when Berkshire was severely affected. The Vicar of Sonning of the time, Thomas de Brackeles, was almost certainly a victim, and perhaps it was he himself who unwittingly carried the infection to Hurst on one of his visits to his flock! It is almost impossible to appreciate, at this distance in time, the horrific destructiveness of the disease. Its ravages were greatest in towns, but the villages were cruelly hit too, and it would not have taken long for a small community such as Hurst to be almost completely obliterated. Of the three to four million who then formed the total population of England, more than half died of the Plague, and Berkshire lost one-third of its people.

Perhaps a pathetic few remained in Hurst, and when the ravages had eased, built new homes a little way off, near the pond which tradition held had been there "since the beginning of time". The pond is fed by a spring, and is presumed to connect underground to the River Loddon.

There must have been a spate of building in the 16th century, including many cottages, the Castle Inn (formerly known as Church House), Hinton House, Stanlake Park, and the earliest part of Haines Hill.

The bowling green is said to have been laid for the benefit of Charles I, in 1628; perhaps this was a favourite visiting place for the king when at Windsor, and it is still much used and enjoyed by the local people.

The tithe barn at Hatch Gate Farm dates back to 1441; the distinctive house High Chimneys in Davis Street reveals the date of its construction by the date "1661" scratched on several bricks.

The Barker family were long connected with the village, and in 1682 William Barker built the one-storeyed almshouses near the church. The school, built in 1843 at a cost of £780, is still used as an infants' school.

The M4 motorway, opened in December 1971, passes through part of the village, but this does not appear to have greatly disturbed the peace, although it has precipitated a great demand for living accommodation within easy reach of London.

Hurst Women's Institute can boast of being the first to be formed in Berkshire. This show of initiative surely cancels out the poor showing of Chaplain Richard, 750 years ago, who ". . . would answer naught of this matter and . . . having been questioned afterwards would not be examined and remained suspended from office . . ."

East Ilsley This old and interesting village lies in a fold of the Downs midway between Abingdon and Newbury, and climbs steeply by narrow winding roads to the top of the hills where the A34 fast road carries the ever-increasing traffic from the Midlands to the south coast.

Its geographical position has determined East Ilsley's part in the pageant of history. The Green Roads of ancient Britain march along the tops of the Downs, and the little brown men of the Bronze Age, the Romans, the Saxons and the medieval countrymen have all worn the tracks with their passing feet.

Because these natural highways brought the wayfarer to East Ilsley it became the centre of a great corn-market in the middle ages. Later the growing wool trade turned it into a famous Sheep Market, to which James I gave royal approval in the early 17th century.

A hundred years ago the annual average sale was 400,000 sheep, and the record was 80,000 penned in a single day, of which 55,000 were sold. Twenty-four inns and public houses catered for the hoards of farmers and shepherds on market days, and the small village was among the busiest corners of Berkshire.

Increasing traffic, man-made roads and new patterns of industry changed the thriving sheep-market into a quiet backwater in the 20th century, and today there are four public houses, a few quiet farms, many cottages, some of great antiquity; several large training stables of racehorses which have achieved national fame, and two early Georgian houses of great beauty that face each other across Broad Street.

A fine village pond is a meeting place near the Rectory, there is a parish church and a Catholic church, several shops, a café, a post office and a police station.

East Ilsley's great asset is the famous Saddler's Shop, three hundred years old and still going strong. The saddler, one of the most skilled craftsmen in the kingdom, is kept at full stretch making saddles for racehorses, hunters, hacks and ponies, and repairing broken and worn leather harnesses. Three local girls work with him, and his wife is his right hand; the saddler even finds time occasionally to talk about his ancient craft to Berkshire Women's Institutes.

A few years ago, East Ilsley was constantly and very sadly in the news. The A34 passed right through this little hillside village, and accidents with crashing lorries and cars became a hideous commonplace. Happily, the new by-pass fast road has freed East Ilsley from its fear and destruction, and now the confident visitors can walk the quiet streets with a tranquil mind. The village has been restored to sanity and its individual charm.

West Ilsley

Into a fold in the bare chalk Downs is tucked the small, well-wooded village of West Ilsley, surprisingly soft and leafy among the rolling hills. A Roman road called the Old Street bounds the parish on the west, and above it the ancient Ridgeway traces its timeless way towards Avebury. The village is a motley of rambling farm houses, old cottages and barns, a few fine houses and a famous training establishment.

All Saints Church, much restored over the centuries, has a charming lych-gate hung about with red roses; and the standard roses on the lawn leading to the porch were given by the Women's Institute to commemorate the fiftieth anniversary of its foundation.

Well placed before the church is a fine cross of peace with a crucifixion and a charming Madonna in its lantern head.

West Ilsley's most colourful churchman, Marc Antonio de Dominus, Archbishop of Spalato, arrived in the reign of James I, having quarrelled with the Roman Church about his unorthodox views. He was made Dean of Windsor and Rector of West Ilsley, and quickly set about making himself as unpopular in England as in Italy. He was described as "fat, irascible, pretentious and very avaricious". He must also have been rather naïve, because he accepted the invitation of Pope Gregory XVth to return to Rome, where he was imprisoned and very soon died. An implacable Inquisition later dug up his body and burnt it with all his writings . . . and possibly the Church lost much by this action, since Marc Antonio was the first person to explain the phenomenon of the rainbow.

His successor, Dr. Godfrey Goodman, also Bishop of Gloucester, entertained Charles I in the Civil War. A rare tract written by one of the King's servants says, "Friday, 8th November, 1644, King Charles marched from Wallingford to West Ilsley (the Bishop of Gloucester 'in Commandam'), at which place he slept that night and on Saturday, the 9th, he went to Donnington Castle and lay at the castle all night".

West Ilsley House, once home of the Morland family, has been divided into flats; but it is a fine Queen Anne house and boasts an authentic powder closet where wigs were once cared for.

About half a mile from the village is Hodcott House, a beautiful building attached to a training establishment for about 80 racehorses. Her Majesty Queen Elizabeth II visits the stables and the village periodically to see some of her own horses in training.

Inkpen lies in the extreme south-west corner of Berkshire, and most of the visitors who come here are looking for Inkpen Beacon, well-known as the highest chalk hill in England (975 feet) and in an area renowned for its outstanding natural beauty.

The Beacon is crowned by Walbury Camp, believed to date from the early Iron Age. The old track which passes along the top of the green downs, through the camp, was there even before the camp was constructed. In those days the hills were the safest places to live, for the marshy lowlands were densely forested and full of dangers. The long barrow on the hill to the west of the camp was the burial place of some of Inkpen's earliest inhabitants.

Today Inkpen's life is scattered over a lowland district over four miles long and nearly as wide in a collection of hamlets— Upper Green, Lower Green and Great Common being the largest. They are on the same sites as early Saxon settlements which had houses grouped round a green (though Inkpen's greens are now enclosed and cultivated). The name of the village is of Saxon origin—Pen was a Saxon word meaning stockade or enclosure and Inga was the Saxon chief who owned it. Some of the large fields have Saxon associations, especially the one still called Haycroft, the name given to the communal hay-field. By the time of the Domesday survey Inkpen had its own mill.

Founder of the church was Roger de Ingpen, whose effigy now rests on the north side of the altar. Its style is so much like that of an effigy of known date in Salisbury Cathedral that it can be attributed to the same period—1220–1250.

When church records began in 1633 the living was held by a rector named Brickenden and members of his family continued to hold office until 1760. In 1695 the Rev. Colwell-Brickenden built the Rectory, now the Old Rectory and used as a private residence. A miniature "William and Mary", it is a beautiful example of the period with gardens in the style of Versailles.

The Butlers succeeded the Brickendens and there was a Butler at the church from 1760 until 1933. The family lived at Kirby House, built about 1770, for 100 years and not at the Rectory. In the days of the Rev. John Butler, who was Rector from 1838 to 1895, the church took second place to the stables, and the Rector hunted with the Craven for 72 winters without missing a season. In the time of his son, Henry Dobree Butler, the last of the family, the church was considerably restored and enriched with many treasures. When this greatly loved Rector died, the memorial erected to him was the oak lych-gate, made in the parish by employees at the local sawmills. The rafters were "cleft" in the traditional style and the adze was used instead of the plane.

There are still several thatched cottages in the village and one of the oldest half-timbered houses in Weavers Lane is the only surviving dwelling of a colony of weavers who once flourished there. The village was also well-known for its baskets and there was a basket-maker in the village until the 1950's.

A rope walk in the Folly was used until the end of the 19th century.

Inkpen's best-known craft was pottery. Local clay was used and labourers who worked in Inkpen's clay were given the derisive nickname of "Inkpen Yellowlegs". The heavier types of domestic pottery were made—bread crocks, cream jars and pitchers. The old kiln in Pottery Road went out of use at the beginning of the 20th century when David Buckeridge gave up his work.

But there was a potter in the village about 2000 B.C. In a sand-pit near Totterdown an early beaker was discovered which is the tallest ever found in the British Isles. There was also an unusual bowl standing on four feet. These unique treasures are in safe keeping in Newbury Museum.

Inkpen's other claim to historical fame is the Gibbet—a landmark for miles around. The first to be erected on this hilltop site was put up in 1676 when George Broomham of Combe (a hamlet on the south side of the hills) and Dorothy Newman of Inkpen were hanged for the murder of the man's wife and son. It was the only time it was used and the original gibbet rotted away, a second was struck by lightning and a third lasted nearly 100 years until it came down in a gale in 1949. The hill looked bare and unfamiliar without a gibbet and by popular request and public subscription a new one was erected with great ceremony in May 1950. The gibbet was made from an oak tree in the village by Mr. F. D. Carter, an employee at the Saw Mills for over 50 years. However, between 1950 and 1969 the gibbet was felled twice by vandals, but repaired and replaced each time.

In 1948 a film, "Black Legend", telling the story of the murders, was written, produced and directed by Alan Cooke and John Schlesinger with local people in its cast. The film was lost in transit in 1971, when it was being returned to the British Film Institute in London by post, after being shown at a local function.

Inkpen used to have three blacksmiths' shops and a village Pound, now the site of Pound Cottages.

The village war memorial is a seven-acre Playing Field, opened in 1947.

Kennington

Lying between Abingdon and Oxford, Kennington is no longer strictly a village . . . its population has grown from 350, a mere hamlet, in 1925 to an area of suburbia, housing over 5,000 in 1979.

Early in this century a fire destroyed most of the old cottages in the village, but there still remains the restored old bakehouse, now known as Woodbine House. Though bereft of ancient buildings, Kennington is rich in local legends . . . in 1762 two local worthies, one happily called Hen-Toe, fought each other for hours on both banks of the Isis until Hen-Toe gave in, and it was reported that "we hear he is since dead". In 1786 Mr. Broom of Kennington sold his wife for 5 shillings to a Littlemore man called Pantin, who led his purchase away with a halter round her neck. Later he repented of his bargain and gave her away to the woodman of Bagley Woods!

In 1893 the decomposed body of an unknown woman was found in Bagley Woods and some Kennington men laconically remembered seeing a man kick a woman in the jaw and threaten to "do for her". These were obviously the good old days.

A happier story, recorded in the old farm books of the Mundys of Manor Farm, tells how the Great Western train came to a halt in the village to find deep floods in all directions. The year was 1852, and the distinguished passengers had to be lifted out and taken by a two-horse farm wagon through the swirling waters to Oxford. There were several heads of Oxford colleges packed into the primitive cart, and best of all, the great engineer Isambard Kingdom Brunel, designer and builder of the railway.

Kingston Bagpuize & Southmoor

These two ancient villages were merged into one civil parish on 1st April, 1971. Once quite separate and spread along the A420 between Oxford and Faringdon, in-filling, new estates and modern housing have physically linked two old rivals and made them one.

The splendid name Kingston Bagpuize has Saxon origins . . . Kingston was a King's Fort on the Wessex border with Mercia; and a Norman Knight, Ralph de Bachepuise, was granted the Manor after the Conquest and has given his name to the village. Spelling has varied greatly over the centuries and there is a 16th-century tapestry map in the Victoria and Albert Museum which calls the place Kingston Baptiste.

Southmoor is sometimes known as Draycott Moor; the southern boundary of the parish is the little River Ock, and the northern boundary the River Thames, where the New Bridge takes one over to Oxfordshire. Needless to say, the bridge is very old, and though its origins are obscure it is thought that it was new in 1416.

In 1970 Kingston Bagpuize celebrated its millenium with a week of junketings, from a ball, a fête, and a barn dance to an exhibition of historical costumes by the Women's Institute; a thousand years of history that commenced in 970 with its first recorded land charter from King Edgar to Britheah. The manor was held by the Bachepuise family until 1299, and later by the Lattons, the Fettiplaces and the Blandys.

The church was built in 1799, in the Italian Renaissance style, and in the 19th century a Methodist chapel was added; both church and chapel now serve a population of about 2,000 people.

The great glory of the village is Kingston House, a fine 17th-century building in the style of Inigo Jones. The beautiful gardens are open to the public at stated times, and are regarded as a botanist's delight, with many rare plants and trees.

From 1863 until 1936 Kingston Bagpuize was the centre of the Old Berks. Hunt, which brought distinguished visitors including the Prince of Wales (later the Duke of Windsor), and great prosperity and colour to the village.

Patterns of life in the parish are now greatly changed, with newcomers filling the housing estates and a successful mingling of old and new in the social life of the place.

KENNET

Kintbury, located between Newbury and Hungerford, stands on the south, sharply rising side of the Kennet Valley.

The earliest known settlement at Kintbury is the Saxon burial ground near the school. This is assumed to be the "Holy Place" referred to by a Saxon lord of the district in A.D. 93. In the Domesday Book the name is Cynetanbyrig and lists a mill on the River Kennet as being worth 4s. or 20p. The original village was sited above the flood level of the Kennet near the present church, which dates from the 12th century with many later additions and alterations. The tower and Norman doorway work survived these alterations. In the church are some fine 18th-century monuments, including one to Sir Jennett Raymond by Scheemakers. The chequerwork of flint and stone on the upper stage of the tower is a very attractive feature of the village, contrasting with the almost universal red brick and tiled roofs of the cottages, occasionally interspersed with slate and thatch.

During the 14th to 16th century, Kintbury village was the main settlement of the Hundred of Kintbury Eagle, which stretched from Letcombe Regis in the north to Shalbourne in the south, and from Hungerford in the west to Enborne in the east. This was a Royal Hundred owned by the King in person; it was given to his Lords for services rendered and sometimes taken back.

The Parish of Kintbury was comprised of seven Manors, the land and lordship of Kintbury Eaton, Templeton, Titcombe held by the sejeanty for keeping one of the King's hawks, Balsdon, Inglewood and Wallingtons and the two detached Manors of Denford and Anvilles. The Manor of Kintbury Amesbury, thenceforth known as Barton Court, was bought by Phillip Jennett, a London brewer; his family and their descendants, the family of Jennett Raymond, held the Manor until 1790, when it passed by descent and marriage to the Dundas family,

In the next 50 years this family provided public life with a well-known Admiral and a Member of Parliament for Berkshire, Charles Dundas, Lord of the Manor of Kintbury, later becoming Lord Amesbury, dying in 1832. The family sold the property to Sir Richard Sutton Estates in 1875 and part of it still remains in Sir Richard's hands. Barton Court, however, after being for years the home of the late Lord Burnham, the Minister of Education of "Burnham Scale" fame, became a preparatory School. It is now a private residence again. Part of the adjoining land is worked for gravel.

Kintbury in the 16th century was a thriving settlement far larger than Hungerford at that time. It had a weekly market and two fairs, one on the feast of the Virgin Mary and another on the feast of St. Simon and St. Jude.

Agriculture was, and still is, the main industry in the area, although chalk was dug at many small quarries in preparation for whiting. Until recently there was a small whiting industry and two brick and tile factories. These have now gone, leaving only disused chalk quarries and the name and buildings of Kiln Farm. The village had three water mills and one silk mill in the early 19th century.

The effects of the Industrial Revolution in Agriculture were felt in Kintbury, and in 1830 the village momentarily acquired a little wider notoriety. Agricultural machinery was introduced into West Berkshire, and this was accompanied by a serious outbreak of rioting, rick-burning and the destruction of new machinery. A detachment of Grenadier Guards was sent from London to help local Yeomanry, led by Lord Craven, Lord Dundas and Captain Houblon, to quell the riots. The party assembled in Newbury then marched on Kintbury, and the ringleaders were arrested to the number of 100. Most of them were found in the Blue Ball public house, which was the rioters' headquarters. One man was executed at Reading, some were transported and many more imprisoned.

The Kennet and Avon Canal was opened through Kintbury in

1812, and, thanks to the Kennet and Avon Canal Trust, is once again navigable up to Kintbury and westwards.

The Rev. Fulwar Craven Fowle, a relative of the Craven family and incumbent of Kintbury for 40 years at the turn of the 18th century, is reputed to have been described by George III as "the best preacher and the best rider to hounds in my whole County of Berkshire". He is remembered now, however, for his connection with Jane Austen. Her sister Cassandra was engaged to Craven Fowle's son, and there were other ties between the two families. In her letters Jane Austen writes several times of her visits to Kintbury, the last being in 1816, the year before she died.

There is only one traceable village legend, that of the Kintbury Great Bell; and one ghost. The bell legend is that a great storm destroyed the church tower and hurled the bell into the river. A wizard prescribed that it should be recovered by passing a chain through a hook fixed to the head of the bell, and then the chain was to be pulled by twelve white heifers, led in moonlight by twelve maidens arrayed in white with red sashes. No word was to be spoken or the chain would break. All went well until the Kintbury witch cried:

> Here comes the great Kintbury bell
> In spite of all the devils in hell.

This broke the spell, the chain snapped and the bell fell back into the river.

The ghost is Lieutenant Dexter's. He asked to be buried with his sword beside him. This sword is said to rattle when people pass through the churchyard at night.

Knowl Hill

Knowl Hill has a population of 700 and is 30 miles from London. The Bath Road (A4) passes through the village. The name is derived from "The Knolle", a hill on the south side crowned by a clump of trees. Extensive views of the countryside can be seen from here, including Windsor Castle. In 1315 a grant of a piece of land at "La Cnolle" is mentioned in a charter of St. Mary's Priory, Hurley.

At one time Knowl Hill was part of Windsor Forest. Records from excavations show that there was once a Roman settlement here, as much Roman pottery has been found. The Bath stage coach rattled through the village till railways killed the industry. Travellers called at the local inns for rest and refreshment while the horses were changed. The farriers' and wheelwrights' premises are still in existence, now two cottages. In their front walls the outline of the archways through which the coaches would pass are still visible. It is interesting that a modern garage on the opposite side of the road continues the tradition of serving travellers. A frequent bus service through the village connects London, Maidenhead and Reading.

Knowl Hill is chiefly agricultural but it has a brick and tile industry which has been owned by the same family for over 100 years.

St. Peter's Church was consecrated in 1841, and was designed by J. C. Buckler of Oxford. He was runner-up to Sir Charles Barry in the competition for the design for the Houses of Parliament. The church was enlarged in 1870.

Cricket is a flourishing village sport. It has been played in the same field since 1890. A yearly Steam and Vintage Vehicle Rally and Fair has been organised lately to raise funds to build a new village hall.

Leckhampstead

One of the most pleasing places in the Downlands, the village sits high above the Wantage to Newbury Road and is built round a small green. On the outskirts is a Bronze Age barrow, cared for by the Ministry of Works.

The original Saxon church dedicated to St. Edmund was demolished in 1860, but items that were saved for the present building are a Jacobean pulpit, a 13th-century font and the altar rails. The Methodist Church still flourishes, but a Wesleyan Chapel has been converted into a private house.

The old manor house is now known as Yew Tree Cottage . . . an attractive 16th-century thatched house. A farmhouse built 200 years later is now known as the Manor. Twenty Leckhampstead houses are listed as "buildings of architectural or historical interest".

An unusual War Memorial is a clock with hands made of bayonets, machine-gun ammunition marks the minutes and the Roman numerals are rifle ammunition. Shell cases rest on staddle stones surrounding the memorial, and the chain linking the stones belonged to a battleship which fought at the Battle of Jutland.

Letcombe Bassett

Take your camera when you go to Letcombe Bassett, for here the timber-framed thatched cottages are mellow and unselfconscious, fitting beautifully into a harmonious whole.

The Ridgeway is only a short walk uphill, and strings of race-horses are a familiar sight in the village and on the Downs. It is fitting that the only public house, The Yew Tree, has a working smithy attached to it.

There is a small church, rather insignificant from outside, but a little gem within and well worth a visit.

Letcombe Bassett has two interesting literary associations. The Old Rectory, a fine Queen Anne house, has a three-hundred-years-old mulberry tree in the garden, under which Dean Swift sat to write when he visited the Rector. One would like to think of *Gulliver's Travels* coming out of Letcombe Bassett Rectory garden, but it was probably one of the Dean's more vitriolic attacks on the government.

The other delightful literary allusion is near the famous water-cress beds, where a thatched cottage on the brook is identified with "Arabella's Cottage" in "Cresscombe", from the Thomas Hardy novel, *Jude the Obscure*.

Letcombe Regis

As the name implies, this is a village with royal associations . . . the Old Manor existed in the time of Edward the Confessor, and King John used it as a hunting lodge. There are two other manors today —Antwicks Manor, a 19th-century house on an older site, and Letcombe Manor, late Georgian, now occupied by the Agricultural Research Council. The beautiful wooded slopes by the brook, and two lakes, greatly enhance the manor grounds.

Letcombe Regis has many variations of architectural styles, from the Victorian Old Vicarage, the Georgian and neo-Georgian houses, and some beautifully placed timber and thatch cottages, which blend most happily along the winding main road.

Above the village, on the Downs, lies the well-preserved vallum and fossa of Segsbury Camp, which is reputedly even older than Uffington's famous White Horse.

The Greyhound public house, on the steps of which the Riot Act is supposed to have been read for the last time in England, is interesting for its early 19th-century brickwork, using a Flemish bond with black glazed headers.

Like its sister village, Letcombe Regis has its stable yards and training establishments, and maintains its racing tradition.

Littlewick Green was recognised as a Common by the White Waltham Enclosure Act of 1807, but the name first appears about the year 1050. A Roman settlement was discovered by aerial photography in a field known as Black Vere. Archaeologists followed up this lead and unearthed Roman relics, proving that Littlewick Green has a long, though perhaps not a spectacular, history.

The visitor will be impressed by the serenity and freedom from haste that is apparent when he views the extensive village green although not 200 yards from the unheeding traffic rushing along the A4. The Green is fringed with thatched cottages, mellow brick houses, the village church, a former chapel, the village hall, and appropriately enough an inn called the Cricketers beneath the shade of an old walnut tree.

The church was built in 1887 by Fanny Ellis, primarily to provide a burial ground at Littlewick. For generations the coffins were carried down the bridle path leading to White Waltham, to be interred in their churchyard. The church has recently acquired a treasure of great interest. It is a 15th-century tempora painting copied by an unknown artist, and found in the coach-house of the Electricity Board's H.Q. at Woolley Hall.

Woolley Hall was the home of George Dunn, from 1886 until his death in 1912. He was an expert on four different subjects—astronomy, arboriculture (the trees he planted are a feature of the Hall), horology and old books. His library was sold at Sothebys after his death for £32,000. It is said that George Dunn suffered from a broken romance. On the morning before his wedding day, his bride-to-be ran away with his brother. The wedding breakfast, which was laid ready, was left untouched all his life.

Formerly a Fair called the "Hope Benefit" was held on bank holidays. Donkeys brought here from the New Forest could be bought for £1. Ashley Hill dominates the local scene and gives rise to the weather rhyme:

When Ashley Hill begins to smoke
Then Shottesbrooke begins to soak.

Shottesbrooke, just south of the village, is famous for its fine 14th-century church, inspired by Salisbury Cathedral with its beautiful slender spire rising from the centre of the cruciform design. Sir William Trussell built it, and the story goes that he was "a worthy old knight addicted to drinking". He nearly died of his excesses, but recovered by taking "water drenches, and water stupes; water gruels and water soups", to everyone's amazement. His wife, a pious lady, so troubled his conscience and tortured his soul that on his recovery

"An oath he sware,
To his lady fair,
'By the cross on my shield
A church I'll build',
And therefore the deuce a form
Is so fit as the cruciform.
And the patron saint that I find the aptest
Is that holiest water-saint, John the Baptist!"

(From the *Berks. Book of Song and Rhyme*)

Another tale concerns a local smith. On the completion of the church in 1337, he climbed the spire to affix the weather-vane. Arrived at the top, he demanded a pot of ale with which to drink the health of the King. The ale was delivered to him, but unfortunately his sense of balance was not equal to his excess of loyalty and he fell to his death. His grave, the first in the churchyard, was dug where he fell, and on his tombstone was inscribed two O's, all he uttered as he fell!

Ivor Novello, who lived at Red Roofs, was another personality who found the tranquillity of Littlewick Green to his taste, and it is here that he wrote "Perchance to Dream".

Littleworth

Here is a village with a royal history. Before his defeat in 1066 King Harold owned 31 hides of land (3,720 acres) at Worth, which passed to Norman William the Conqueror, and later to the Abbey of Abingdon.

The Knights of St. John of Jerusalem, also called the Knights Hospitallers, a religious order of chivalry, owned the land in the middle ages, and as late as 1834 there is mention of a Henry James being appointed as a Tithingman of Hospital.

Littleworth came back to the Crown in the reign of Henry VI and that pious educationist promptly gave it to Oriel College, Oxford; the College still is patron of the living of Littleworth Church, but has sold off all the land.

The church itself has only existed since 1839. Before that, parishioners had to walk two miles to Faringdon on a Sunday, until Edward Bouverie Pusey decided that the villagers were poor and godless and needed their own church. This was built with money given by his Oxford friends, and was followed by a Primitive Methodist Chapel in 1891, and a small Mission room at Thrupp.

Littleworth remains very much as it has looked for a hundred

91

years . . . only six houses have been built since the war; but with the recently installed main drainage the village looks forward to a more expansive future.

Longcot

One of the complaints of visitors to the Vale of the White Horse is the difficulty of actually seeing the horse. He prances up on the top of the curving Downs, and there are relatively few spots, except from a helicopter, where one can get a clear view. But from the village of Longcot there are many places where the horse can be properly seen . . . looking, to be sure, rather more catlike than equine, but a splendid prehistoric creature for all that.

Longcot, with a population of about 300, saw its heyday in the 19th century, when a branch of the Wilts. & Berks. Canal flowed by with its barges filled with coal, grain and wool for Witney blankets. The canal has gone, but the village is once again on the increase, with some new housing, a bus service to Oxford and Swindon, and the Royal Military College of Science almost on its doorstep at nearby Shrivenham.

There are many attractive stone-built and thatched cottages and a 13th-century church. Like many another church tower, Longcot's needs urgent repairs, and the excellent peal of bells can no longer be rung. The Reverend John Hughes, a much-loved Vicar in the last century, was a brother of the author of *Tom Brown's Schooldays,* who lived in the neighbouring parish of Uffington. In the church is a brass plaque to the memory of the Reverend and Mrs. Carter, who drowned in the *Titanic* shipwreck; Mrs. Carter was a niece of the Hughes brothers.

In the churchyard is the sad little grave of a 14-year-old boy who was frozen to death in a blizzard on the downs in 1881.

Another well-known member of the Hughes family, Miss May Hughes, became known as the Angel of Whitechapel for her social work among the poor in the East End of London. Her home, Rest Cottage, was a haven for ailing children, who also spent health-giving holidays with village families.

In the garden of Rest Cottage Miss Hughes built a hut called The Ark, which was used as a village hall for many years, and is now a youth club. She also started a coffee house in a cottage on the Green with the aim of keeping the villagers out of the public houses.

Longcot has had three schools in its history . . . first a Charity

School where pupils paid one penny a week; then a village school on the Green; and now, on the same site, one of the finest modern schools in the county.

Marcham, like many villages in this part of the old county, was once part of the great Abbey of Abingdon, given to the church by the Saxon King Egbert, and the old church tower dates from this time.

The church is late medieval, and well worth a visit; in the great days of the Abbey there were 7 dovecotes in the village, indicating a prosperous place and many mouths to be fed.

In 1538, with the Dissolution of the Monasteries, Marcham and its rich farmlands and Tudor houses passed into the ever-open hands of Henry VIII, and later came into the possession of the Elwes family.

Marcham rejoices in endless colourful legends of the 18th-century John Elwes, man of wealth and taste, traveller, member of parliament, eccentric and miser. His hat was lifted from a scarecrow, he claimed to have spent 1 shilling and 6 pence on his election expenses, and when he was dying his lawyer was made to draw his will by firelight to save the cost of a candle.

John Elwes' granddaughter, Emily, made a runaway marriage with Thomas Duffield, a local farmer who later became an M.P. The Duffield family rebuilt Marcham Park in its present Georgian form, and this fine house is now W.I. property, Denman College of Further Education for Women's Institute members from all over England and Wales.

Marcham is a grey stone village, very mellow and attractive, with the addition of well-planned modern housing estates, including a number of homes for the elderly and a very handsome Church Institute where various meetings are held.

Marcham Priory is an interesting house, partly 16th century on an earlier foundation, and once a rest house for Abingdon Abbey. Like many other old church properties, it is reputed to be haunted, in the most benevolent and comfortable way; a previous tenant has assured me that footsteps go up and down the stairs and corridors where no person can be seen.

Another house, Hyde Farm, built about 1600, is generally supposed to have been given to James Hyde, executioner of King Charles I, as a reward for his professional services.

Marcham Mill Barn is mentioned in Domesday Book, but is now modernised and a comfortable private house.

Across the salt marshes between Marcham and the River Ock, wild sea celery grows, and it is claimed that the name Marcham means "The Village of Wild Celery".

COTHILL, on the outskirts of Marcham, has an attractive handful of old cottages and houses, a handsome preparatory school for boys, Cothill House, and is the site of a National Nature Reserve, and two nature reserves owned by the Berks, Bucks, and Oxon Naturalists Trust. Permission is needed to visit these reserves.

FRILFORD, close to Marcham, is mainly noted for the Golf Course and fine Clubhouse, set among pine trees on sandy soil. The houses around the links are modern and sometimes opulent, but the A338 road that passes through Frilford is reputedly an old Roman Road. There are two notable inns in the district that cater for the carriage-trade . . . The Dog House, where on a summer evening the Morris Dancers can sometimes be seen; and the Noah's Ark, a humble little village pub that has been given a new lease of life with a complete face-lift and a restaurant of international standard.

GARFORD, in the same area, has some attractive old houses, and notably an interesting 13th-century church, or St. Luke's Chapel. Electricity has not long been brought into the church, which retains its beautiful big candle holders, and has a fine wooden screen of 15th-century workmanship.

MILTON MANOR

Milton Midway between the villages of Drayton, Steventon and Sutton Courtenay, this old settlement can claim a thousand years of history, and its original Saxon name, Middeltune, obviously derives from its geographical position. In A.D. 956 Edwy the Fair gave fifteen hides of land (roughly 1,200 acres) to Alfwin, who later conveyed it to the Abbey of Abingdon. The chapel, built in the reign of William Rufus, was Abbey property, and the first rector was appointed in 1325 by Edward II.

The delightful church today is of later vintage and is dedicated to St. Blaise, patron of woolcombers, as is fitting in a village once the centre of the wool-growing trade, and on the route to the great sheep fair at Ilsley.

Collectors of tombstones will like the many beautifully carved examples in the little quiet churchyard—there is a handsome stone dated 1764. Milton has had a tradition of stone carving for the last 200 years, and a member of the same family can still be found at the old stonemason's shop. After the Great War, over 300 headstones were carved in this village and sent to France for the graves of the local families' war dead.

Right in the middle of this lovely place is Milton Manor, designed in the manner of Inigo Jones in a beautiful faded rose-pink brick, and placed with calm perfection in a setting of tall trees, green lawns and ornamental lake. Milton Manor is opened to the public at stated times.

In 1546 the Calton family was in possession, but it was sold in 1768 to John Bryant Barrett, ancestor of the present owner.

At the gates of the manor the village public house displays its sign . . . The Admiral Benbow. This famous sailor has a link with Milton House . . . his daughter married one of the Calton family. When Peter the Great, Czar of Russia, visited England on his famous fact-finding voyage, he stayed at Milton House, undoubtedly through his passionate interest in ships, dockyards and the sea, and the Admiral was a great source of information. The Admiral's sword is still at Milton House, and his portrait hangs in the village pub.

Another royal visitor was William of Orange in 1688. After his landing at Brixham the great little Dutchman marched his army north through Newbury and spent a night at Milton House while his 20,000 men were quartered in Abingdon.

On the outskirts of this attractive village Milton Depot was established by the Army and flourished for many years. The site has now been sold to a company for warehousing, and 120 people from the surrounding district are employed there.

Milton North Field has yielded up some archaeological treasures . . . there are traces of a Saxon burial ground, and in 1832 a very fine Saxon Fibula, worked in gold and jewelled with garnets, was dug up. It can now be seen in the Ashmolean Museum, Oxford.

The old church school in the village bears this inscription: "A.D. 1796. This school was erected and endowed by J. O. Warner, Rector of this Parish, for educating poor children and bringing them up to fear the Lord".

There is a beautiful walk from Milton to Steventon beside the Ginge Brook and leading to the Causeway. By road to Milton Hill the way is garlanded with cherry orchards, with apples and pears and soft fruit in two large fruit farms, and at any time of year Milton is a pleasant place to visit.

The Moretons

North and South Moreton lie at the centre of a circle enclosed by Wallingford, Wittenham Clumps, Didcot and Blewburton Hill, and traces of a Roman road skirt the eastern side of both villages.

Take your camera when you go to North Moreton . . . its winding main street is scattered all along with beautiful old cottages and some fine brick houses of great antiquity. The village has suffered less from in-filling than most in this flat plain of Berkshire, and looks much as it has done for centuries.

The Church of All Saints mainly dates from 1270, but has a 15th-century tower and a late Norman font. The interesting Stapleton Chantry, with an especially fine east window, commemorates the Stapleton family who held the Manor in the 13th to 15th centuries. A Stapleton fell at Bannockburn and another was a Judge of the King's Bench.

The family at the Manor in the 16th and 18th centuries were the Dunches, related to Oliver Cromwell. There is a nonconformist tradition in the village where a Methodist Chapel existed from the mid-19th century to the mid-20th century.

A truly rural and mainly farming countryside, North Moreton has an interesting example of "domestic" industry expanding into a large-scale enterprise. In 1938 the marketing of eggs from the surrounding farms grew into Thames Valley Eggs Ltd., with a "station" in the village and twenty others in the area. In 1971 the firm distributed 866 million eggs with a turnover of £13 million.

The New Victoria Inn sits at the north end of the village, and is relatively modern; its predecessor, the Old Victoria, is now an attractive private house. At the other end of the long village street is the Bear, a tiny and ancient hostelry that adjoins the Cricket Club. Cricket is taken very seriously in the Moretons, and the club was founded in 1858.

SOUTH MORETON, the larger of the two Moretons, once possessed four Manors, but there are only slight indications now of two of them—Adresham and Fulscot. Sandesville Manor remains a fine late 15th-century building, probably very similar to the old Manor of North Moreton. The Manor of Bray can also be seen, and there is a wealth of fine cottages and old houses all along the village street.

The Church of St. John the Baptist dates mainly from the 13th and 14th centuries, though the south and west walls are Norman and there are clear marks of a Saxon west door. Outside is an ancient yew tree, traditionally thought to have housed bows and arrows during church service.

Certainly, villagers who failed to practise their archery were fined in the year 1628, and in the Civil War men of Moreton fell in battle and are said to be buried in a mound near St. John's Church.

There is a Baptist Chapel, built in 1832.

South Moreton, too, has its greatly expanded "domestic" industry. The firm of A. C. Hedges Ltd. with its headquarters locally grew up from the 1920's onwards to become a major distributor of meat products in the north of Berkshire and to its own chain of London shops.

Mortimer

"On 8th before Kalends of October Aegalward son of Kypping was laid in this place.
Blessed be he who prays for his Soul
Toki wrote this."

This inscription, on a Saxon tombstone in Mortimer, pinpoints one year in the very early history of the village—A.D. 994. For it was in that year that Aegalward is mentioned in the *Saxon Chronicle*. Aethelweard, or Aegalward, was an historian, first translator of the *Chronicle*, consequently a man of influence. Kypping, his father, was Lord of the Manor of Mortimer. Toki, who apparently erected the stone, was a wealthy courtier in the reign of Canute, who was proclaimed King of England in 1017 and who divided the country into the four earldoms of Northumbria, East Anglia, Mercia and Wessex. His reign, lasting until 1035, was one of peace and prosperity, so no doubt Toki took advantage of the lull in hostilities to put up a worthy monument to this learned man of the previous century. Presumably Toki was also a Mortimer man.

The first village church was burnt down during the Danish invasion, possibly in A.D. 871, when ". . . the Danes had possession of the place of slaughter. And in the course of the year nine general engagements were fought against the host in the kingdom to the south of the Thames. . . ." A second church was built on the same site and added to over the years, and the present church was built over the foundations of the two earlier ones in 1869.

Although the present bells were hung in the 17th century, recast in 1709 and again in 1896 when two new ones were added, the peal has echoes of that shadowy early church, for metal from the original bells was incorporated in the later ones.

Unfortunately a fire in the Parish Clerk's house destroyed the earliest Parish Registers, but the remaining ones dating from 1681 are in an excellent state of preservation, giving valuable insight into village life of the time.

Great Park and Little Park, two thriving farms, were part of the marriage portions given by Henry VIII to five of his wives— Catherine of Aragon, Anne Boleyn, Jane Seymour, Catherine Howard and Catherine Parr. Why poor Anne of Cleeves was left out is not known!

In 1588, Mortimer resident Stephen Cane died, leaving estate valued at £28 6s. 5d. to be divided amongst his 12 relatives! At least this was easier to implement than many wills of the time, when perhaps one sheep or cow might be bequeathed to a whole family, members being scattered over a wide area.

Highways and commons in the parish tell a clear story of by-gone days and outdated customs. Welshman's Way was the path along which the Welsh drovers trudged behind their small, tough ponies and shaggy cattle, arriving for the Mortimer Horse and Welsh Cattle Fair on November 6th. Horse Fairs abounded in the early days, and at the larger fairs as many as 45,000 animals would come under the hammer at the same time. The fairs were the "big events" of the year for country folk, and a usually quiet village could be transformed overnight into a medley of colour, noise, hard bargaining, entertainment and excitement.

Goodboys Lane was called after a family of that unusual name who were freeholders in 1540; a road was cut in 1805–6 near the old windmill . . . the sails no longer creak in the wind but Windmill Road is still there; the Forehead, leading to Beech Hill, was known in 1512 as Fair Mead or Front Meadow; Butlers Lane re-calls Thomas Botiller, who owned the land in 1467; Five Oakes, originally Five Oak Glade, crops up in 16th-century documents; Gibbet Piece recalls a darker side of life—the execution of two young men, in 1787, for the murder of the village carrier. Their bodies remained, hung in chains, as an awful warning, until old Madame Brocas of Wokefield had them taken down. Those very chains, made by local blacksmith Mr. Davis, are now in Reading Museum. Hammonds Heath, tradition tells, is a corruption of "Amen Heath", so named because at one time the parish clerk had right of pasture and wood-cutting. Is this, perhaps, the origin of the many other country names including "Amen"? Pickling Yard, close to an old Roman encampment, is a modern name having been used as a place for tarring the ends of telegraph poles.

In 1780 the introduction of threshing machines caused wide-spread alarm in the countryside and the wrecking of the machines. Six leaders of riots in Mortimer were punished as an example to other troublemakers, three being deported, three executed.

In 1805, at the time of the enclosure award, 20 acres now known as Fair Ground, in the centre of the village, were allotted to the vicar and other trustees for the benefit of the poor of the district. Certain rights entitled the parishioners to take gravel, and cut turf and small timber in various places on Brewery Common and Burnt Common.

In 1901, school dinners were served to 94 children at the charge of 1d. per head. Four years later it was reported that, as a collecting ground for butterflies and moths, Mortimer was perhaps as good a place as any in the south of England; species found in abundance included Purple Emperor, White Admiral, Wood White, Large Tortoiseshell, Duke of Burgundy, Silver Washed Fritillary, Holly Blue, Chalk Hill Blue, Death's Head Hawk and Convolvulus Hawk.

Now, 70 years later, 1d., or even 1p, would not go far towards a dinner, and Mortimer's butterflies and hawks are fighting a losing battle against the wonders of modern science!

Mortimer West End

Although this village is just within the boundaries of Hampshire, it has from earliest times been a tithing of the Berkshire village of Stratfield Mortimer, and its fortunes linked with the royal county.

Situated in old Common lands the southern boundary of Mortimer is the ancient Roman road to Silchester, and its westernmost point is marked by an old boundary stone called the Impstone.

The parish church of St. Saviour was built as a gift from Mr. Richard Benyon in 1856, and an older Congregational Chapel was built in 1798 by two friends who are buried side by side near the chapel.

John Whitburn, a young turf-cutter, was converted and became a local preacher in 1778. One of his converts was Mr. John Mulford, a wealthy eccentric who came from a family of mole-catchers, and claimed that "one of his ancestors was mole-catcher to William the Conqueror".

John Whitburn gave the land, and John Mulford, with some help from the villagers, erected the chapel. Whitburn died in 1803 and his friend was buried beside him in 1814, at the age of 93.

It is recorded that old John Mulford looked out of his window on a January day and said, "A fine day for the gossips to go about and say 'Old Mulford is dead!' " With which remark he quietly died.

A succession of devoted ministers kept the chapel going, notably the first Pastor, Mr. Andrew Pinell, and then his son, Charles Pinell, who died in June 1897, having between them guided their parishioners for a period only six years short of a century.

Sadly enough, the little chapel, which called forth so much devotion from local men, is now falling into decay.

Moulsford

Snug beside the River Thames and along the road from Wallingford to Reading lies this charming small village, and there is no finer port of call than the Beetle and Wedge Hotel. Here the river boats tie up, crews shop at the river store and buy petrol, with the brimming river winding away to Streatley or Wallingford. The towpath to Streatley makes a pleasant place to stroll and watch the little boats go by.

There are only 400 people living in Moulsford, but it has two good private schools and a nursing home, and the 17th-century Manor is now a training school for nurses attached to Fairmile Hospital.

Coins, pottery, rings and brooches from Roman and Saxon times have been found locally, and in 1960 a Bronze Age Torque was ploughed up in the recreation field. It weighed one pound, and is made of gold . . . you can see it in Reading Museum.

The small church stands in the Manor grounds and was once privately owned. Moulsford was a Chapelry of Cholsey, and its history has been linked with this nearby village. But Moulsford has remained peaceful and rural, with old half-timbered cottages and flower-filled gardens running down to the water, while Cholsey has plunged into the 20th century.

Northcourt

Once a Manor of Norecott and part of the Benedictine Abbey of Abingdon, later a village called Northcote, this old corner of Berkshire has now been engulfed by the spreading town of Abingdon.

History remains in the stones and soil, but the old buildings are gone, with one noble exception. The old Tithe Barn that belonged to the Abbey, and was built about 1270, has been rescued, restored, and converted into a splendid church.

Much of the conversion was a labour of love, time and talents being voluntarily given by a great number of people, including residents and students from the A.E.R.E. Hostel.

Very little structural changes were made, the 17th-century roof was retained, old stone carvings and a cross from the Abbey were incorporated into the fabric, and the pulpit made from stones from the old Abbey Watermill.

The work was largely inspired by the Rev. Mr. Hubbard, curate in charge, who had been an architect. After his departure, the Rev. Mr. John Moore carried on the work, and on November

25th, 1961, the Tithe Barn Church was consecrated by the Bishop of Oxford, and is now called Christ Church.

Northcourt is rightly proud of its beautiful church, in the making of which most of the community has shared.

Padworth

Paedenwurttel—"the settlement of Paeola, by the road"—was the original name of this village. "The road" was one of those built by the Romans, and Grimm's Dyke or Bank, running through the upper part of Padworth, may have been remains of the earthworks of pre-Roman Silchester.

Cloth and flour mills, sheep farming, rod stripping and hoop-cutting were all once carried on at Padworth. Some light industry has replaced some of these old crafts, but the village has changed little over the years, and farming is still the chief occupation today.

The Norman church has a round apse and stone altar, still in use. Roman bricks, no doubt removed from decaying Silchester, are to be found in the building.

The two springs in the village were renowned, like so many in this area, for curing eye diseases.

Clumps of fir trees are said to have been planted at intervals on the parish boundaries, each clump representing one letter of "Padworth". Only the "A" clump retains its name, though the bus company persists in calling it the "Hay Clump".

Back in the 16th century, Elizabeth Brightwell left money in trust to pay a dame to teach the poor children of the village to read and write. Today's school children still benefit from this fund, as do the elderly folk from various old charities. The income of the latter is roughly the same as over 150 years ago, but the 10½ tons of coal it then purchased is now reduced to a mere 8 cwt. An extract from an old account book kept by the charity trustees reads:

1869

Paid to Messers Ayres for 10 ton 12 cwt. of coal £10	1	5
Refreshment to men and carters	3	5
Two men's labour, weighing and distributing coal	3	4
Use of baskets three times...	1	0

There is still a distribution of bread once a year, thanks to a Lady Elizabeth Marvyn, but the old wood-fired bakehouse is no more.

In the autumn of 1643, Parliamentary troops, retiring wearily after the 1st Battle of Newbury, were surprised by Prince Rupert's

Horse in Padworth Gully. Some 300 men perished in this skirmish, and were buried in pits in the churchyard.

The village has a rich store of old sayings, some of the best being:

"Wherever the wind is on Candlemas day,
There it will stay till the end of May."

"Better late than never, but better never late."

"Hi, you, how fur to Tadley, God help us?"

A "bush" is the name for a splinter in the finger; to "terrify" means to tease; "Cheese logs" or "piggies" are woodlice; "efts" or "effets" are newts.

Well-tried old country remedies include goosegrease for chilblains; and for coughs, "Good Friday Bread", that is bread from the Good Friday Sacrament powdered and taken in water; or a substance containing, as its chief ingredient, "hair from a donkey's tail"! Dandelion, parsnip, potato and currant wines are all made locally, as well as sloe gin.

What pictures are conjured up by the old field names! Beachatas, Broad and Lower Halfpenny, Maggysjaw (who was Maggy?), Hag Pit (did they throw the witches in there?), Duck's Nest, Shinbone and Hicky Vicky (probably a corruption of "Aqua Vitae", from the name of the curative spring).

Times have changed since the farmers walked the peaceful lane from Padworth to Reading Market, with their sheep and cattle; but it is said there is still some ghostly contact with those quieter days. Edward Hobbs, Parish Clerk from 1871 until 1911, used to tell of lights that were visible at certain times at night, along that road. They resembled two yellowish carriage lamps and appeared to travel quickly. When almost near, they just disappeared, and a strange uncanny stillness enveloped the watcher—there have been many since Hobbs' time to vouch for this story, and even the rivalling headlamps cannot obscure those mysterious lamps of a bygone age.

RIVER PANG
NR BUCKLEBURY

Pangbourne

Pangbourne is a favoured residential and holiday resort on the junction of the Thames and Pang rivers. Approaching the village from Streatley, the Thames, and Pangbourne reach in particular, is of unsurpassed beauty.

The south branch of the Ridgeway, via Upper Basildon, dropped down into the valley at Pangbourne, where the Thames could be crossed, and there must have been a ford, then a rough bridge at that spot since very early times. The Roman Road from Silchester (Calleva Atrebatum) to Dorchester ran through the parish, where Neolithic, Roman and Saxon remains have been discovered. Interesting finds were made on Shooter's Hill when the railway line was cut in 1839, namely, 40 coins of silver, gold and brass dating A.D. 69 to 383, and many skeletons.

Beorhtwulf, King of Mercia, who was put to flight at Canterbury by the marauding Danes in A.D. 851 granted land, in a Charter dated A.D. 843 to the parish church of St. James the Less. Rebuilt in 1868, leaving the existing brick tower built in 1718, the church houses a Jacobean pulpit and a large collection of hatchments of the Breedon family. There is an interesting monument to Sir John Davies, who won his knighthood at the taking of Cadiz in 1596 and who died in 1625. His effigy, with his two wives and his son and daughter kneeling below, lies at the north-east end of the church. Nearby, there are memorials to three sisters, who died in 1650, 1659 and 1661. Lord Nelson's favourite bo'sun, Tom Carter, lived in Pangbourne and is buried in the churchyard.

Church Cottage, west of the churchyard, was the home of Kenneth Grahame, author of *The Wind in the Willows*, who undoubtedly found inspiration for his classic as he wandered along the ever-changing but always peaceful riverside.

Opposite the church is a row of well-preserved Tudor and 17th-century cottages, and an old smithy.

There are several old inns dating back to the 17th century. Berkshire County Council has designated the centre of the village as a conservation area, under the Civic Amenities Act. The area includes High Street, the Square, and the area immediately around the church.

The fine red brick 18th-century house, Bere Court, is situated in the south-west of the parish. A former building on the site was, originally, a country residence and Chapel of the Abbots of Reading. Later this passed to Sir Francis Englefield, and in 1596 it was bought by Sir John Davies. In 1671 the property passed to John Breedon, who was a great benefactor to the village, and who built and endowed the Breedon School, part of which still stands on the Reading Road. The Breedon Trust still exists to educate boys of the parish.

Pangbourne College adjoins Bere Court land, standing on the hill about a mile from the village. It was founded by Sir Thomas Lane Devitt and his son Philip in 1917 to educate and train boys for the Royal and Merchant Navies. The founders stipulated, however, that the education provided was to be suitable for any boy who subsequently decided not to take up a career at sea. The College owns 100 yards of River Thames frontage, and boathouses and craft of all sizes.

A small area of common land, and the old Cattle Pound, are to be found near Pangbourne College, on the Yattendon road.

A stretch of riverside, known as Pangbourne Meadow, lying to the east of Whitchurch Bridge, is owned by the parish, having been purchased by voluntary contributions in the 1930's. The adjoining portion of the meadow was purchased by the National Trust, and the whole meadow is controlled by the Parish Council.

The Pangbourne sign, which is an attraction to visitors, was erected in Station Road in 1961. It shows Beorhtwulf, with the Charter, and a Saxon ship, over the name of the village. Kenneth Grahame's book, and the symbolic willows, add a modern touch to the design.

Pinkney's Green

derives its name from the Norman Knight, Ghilo de Pinkney, who was granted lands in the Maidenhead area, as reward for supporting William the Conqueror. Many Pinkneys have been lords of the manor, the last being Catherine Pinkney, mother of the illegitimate Peregrine Hoby, who was adopted as heir to the Hoby estates in Bisham.

A dictionary definition of a village as a "settlement of huts round a track of land to which all had common rights of cultivation" describes exactly Pinkney's Green. The "huts" are now well-built residences. When the growth of Maidenhead and the trunk roads threatened the district, the National Trust took over the guardianship of Maidenhead Thicket, known to locals as "The Common". Within living memory, flocks of sheep owned by the local inhabitants grazed there. There is still a house called "Shepherd's Standing" built on land where once the shepherds met to pick out their flocks. The sheep have been replaced by what has been described by an old inhabitant as a "snowfall of geese".

Maidenhead Thicket was first known by its present name in the 13th century when it was called Maidenheath or Maiden-hythe, meaning New Wharf, an easy landing place for Maidens! In the days of coaching, highwaymen hid in this wild and uncultivated part and battened off the travellers. There is a. record as early as 1255 that trees and brushwood were cut back to make the road safer. The Vicar of Hurley is said to have received extra pay for braving the dangers of the Thicket, on his way to take services at Maidenhead. 1838 was the year when the Great Western Railway was opened up between Paddington and Maidenhead, destroying for ever the isolation of Pinkney's Green.

When building threatened an area, the Archaeological and Historical Societies excavated sites, discovering all kinds of medieval and pre-historic objects. As recently as 1964 excavations in an area known as Camley unearthed a potter's field with 11 kilns, four of which have been carefully examined. A variety of interesting domestic pottery sherds have also been found. Other digs have revealed sherds of Belgic origin and even a Palaeolithic hand axe. Robin Hood's Arbour probably refers to the mythical "Green Man", a spirit that inhabits the woods and of pagan origin.

The Maidenhead Brick and Tile Company's kilns were functioning at Pinkney's Green till quite lately. At one time they were owned by Mr. Cooper, who built the remarkable Queen Anne Hotel on Castle Hill (now demolished) as a demonstration of his virtuosity as a brick and tile maker. The brick works them-

selves were considered an interesting example of industrial archaeo-
logy.

Local names suggest links with the past, such as "The Old
Saxon Road" aligning with Malders Lane, which passes through
the old Brick and Tile Company's yard. A magistrates' Court
House once existed on the long Courthouse Road, and the Pond
House commemorates the Reading Pond that is marked on the
old maps of the Bath Road.

Pinkney's Green has another claim to fame in that it was the
actual birthplace of the Girl Guide movement, the first "Troop"
being formed here by Miss Baden-Powell in 1910.

Priestwood was the first "Neighbourhood Centre" of
Bracknell New Town to be developed. Nine
such centres have been planned, each with its own community
centre, church, shops, schools, public house, play spaces and open
rural area. Although Priestwood may not be considered technically
a village, the rural spirit and interest remains. After all, Priestwood began in the wooded S.W. section of the parish of Warfield,
with a tributary of the Kennet, the Bull, passing through it, fed by
Warfield waters.

Today Priestwood is proud of its New Town amenities but has
managed to keep its undulating contours and many well-established
trees. There is now an attractive riverside walk to Binfield along
the Bull. At first we were sad to see farms taken over and Priestwood Common woodlands bulldozed out of existence, but when
the pleasant houses with their pretty gardens and wide, well-
grassed spaces emerged, we were reconciled to our loss, especially
when we saw erstwhile London children playing so healthily and
safely in their new surroundings. The growth of neighbourliness
has been encouraged by the shopping centre and the church, with
its delicate fibreglass spire. St. Andrew's is an exciting new design
allowing a spacious uncluttered nave where the altar is wholly
visible and the priest is one with his congregation, and not segre-
gated as in older churches.

Bracknell Street grew from a small settlement where paths
crossed in Windsor Forest, into a sleepy but prosperous community of about 5,000 inhabitants. Horse fairs were held in April,
August and October all through the 18th and 19th centuries when
bull-baiting was popular. This sport was forbidden after 1835. The
October Fair was also a Hiring Fair where anyone from a cook to
a farm labourer announced their skills for hire. The cooks wore

a red ribbon and carried a basting spoon, and the housemaids put on a blue ribbon and carried a broom. From these fairs sprang the present Cattle and Produce Market. The largest egg market in the South of England founded in 1870 is a Bracknell speciality.

When the Windsor Forest Turnpike Trust was formed in 1759, Bracknell boasted several hostelries for the London stage coaches. Two of the turnpike milestones, proclaiming the distance from Hyde Park Corner, are still to be seen. The Red Lion Inn was one of the original coaching inns, the first stop after the rather dangerous drive from Wokingham through Priestwood Common.

Purley

The Thames-side village of Purley lies astride the A329 Reading to Pangbourne road. There are still two sizeable farms in the parish and one farmer has recently started a vineyard which he hopes to see commercially productive by the mid-70's.

Although, with the exception of the tower, the Church of St. Mary the Virgin was entirely rebuilt in 1870, there is still the original Norman chancel arch and font, unusually carved with the face of Our Lord.

In 1291 the Advowson of the church was valued at £4 6s. 8d., the Abbot of Reading receiving a pension of 2s. A sum of 6s. a year was at one time distributed among poor widows under the heading of "cow money".

Purley Magna—on part of which Purley Park now stands—once belonged to Edward the Confessor and was held by the Huscarle family from about 1166–1379, and then for nearly 300 years by the St. Johns. The arms of Sir John St. John—a staunch Royalist who lost three sons in the Civil War—are engraved on the church tower with the date 1621. On the same wall is an elaborate mural tablet to Anne, first wife of Edward Hyde, later Lord Clarendon, who died 2nd July, 1632, aged 20. She was travelling to Wiltshire with her husband when she became ill at Reading and was taken to relatives at Purley Hall (then known as Hyde Hall). There she died of smallpox in premature confinement and was buried in Purley Church. On the mural she is holding a baby in her arms.

The Roll of Parsons and Rectors of St. Mary's dates back to 1566. A case was brought against the Rev. William Gostwick, Rector in 1711, by George Blagrave ". . . in a pique for not keeping an Bull for ye use of ye Parish". By obtaining the opinion of the Lord Chancellor of Ireland, at considerable expense, the Rector won his case. Later, he quarrelled with a Mrs. Blagrave, for taking clover from his Glebe land.

In the churchyard are the tombs of Thomas Canning, brother of Prime Minister George Canning, and the distinguished artist, Frank Spenlove-Spemlove.

Purley Hall, originally "La Hyde", then "Hyde Hall", was built in 1609 by Francis Hyde and later owned by Edward Hyde, Earl of Clarendon and Lord Chancellor. Eventually the Hydes went into voluntary exile with Charles II in Belgium, and while there Hyde's daughter Anne married Charles II's brother James (afterwards James II), and was mother of Queens Anne and Mary.

James II's coat of arms is emblazoned over the front door at Purley Hall. Portraits of Sarah, Duchess of Marlborough, and James's second wife, Mary of Modena, have hung at the Hall since those days, and also a monogrammed portrait, by Lely, of a young man, possibly James himself, painted whilst the family was still in Belgium.

In 1720 the Hydes sold their heavily mortgaged estate to Francis Hawes, a Customs official. In 1773 it was bought by the Revd. Dr. Henry Wilder, Rector of Sulham.

During Dr. Wilder's ownership, Purley Hall was let to Warren Hastings, former Governor-General of India, who lived there from 1788–1794, while his long trial for alleged corruption was in progress. It is said that he prepared his defence there before being acquitted with honour. He also farmed, bred cattle and horses, and had a large menagerie brought from abroad—his celebrated Indian Zoo. There is still an Elephant Yard at the Home Farm and a small painting in the house shows some of the creatures about the pool below the house.

The ghosts of Warren Hastings and a grey lady or nun were said to haunt Purley Hall. In fact, when Major and Mrs. Bradley first lived there in 1961, the atmosphere was so oppressive that they arranged for a service of exorcism.

Historically, little seems to be actually known about Purley Lodge. Was the house once a minor monastery or priest hole? About eight years ago the present owner, when repairing the kitchen floor, discovered an underground passage running in the direction of the river. Could this be the tunnel once believed to run to Mapledurham on the opposite bank? If so, was it a means of escape or communication for its Catholic Blount family when religious persecution was rampant?

A room simply known as "the Chapel", and a holy water stoup, carved out of the solid wall in a cupboard, add to the mystery.

An eccentric local character was Major Storer, who spied a group of ladies picnicking in the park and, without listening to explanations, threw crockery, cutlery and tablecloth into the river. Whereupon one of the ladies said: "Major Storer, will you please thank your wife for inviting us, and for lending the things you have just thrown into the river!"

In 1948 Purley Park was established as a Home for Handicapped Men, and has continued as such to the present day.

Radley

The Radley district has been inhabited for 3,000 years . . . Bronze and Iron Age, Romano-British and medieval men have all left their traces behind them, and the Ashmolean Museum in Oxford houses relics from the Wick Hall, Barrow Hills and Wick Farm areas near the river.

The 1968 finds are still being examined in the museum's workshops, but notable among those on exhibition are a pair of gold ornaments (probably earrings) and a set of nine 3AE coins from a Romano-British grave.

In the Middle Ages the Manor of Radley belonged to Abingdon Abbey, passing at the Dissolution to Lord Seymour of Stukely, to Princess Elizabeth, to George Stonhouse, of the Royal Household; after 200 years in the Stonhouse family, to the Bowyers. The second Sir George Bowyer leased Radley Hall to Dr. William Sewell of Exeter College, Oxford, who founded St. Peter's College there.

Radley was technically a curacy of St. Helen's, Abingdon, and Radley Church, with its memorials to the Stonhouses and Bowyers, its unusual oaken pillars and nave arches, its interesting canopied pulpit, and the misericords in the chancel, is described by Sir John Betjeman as having "a sense of mysterious richness".

In 1844 the Oxford–Didcot railway cut Radley in two. The little station became the junction for Abingdon. Victorian housing for railway workers and jobs for the villagers came with the trains,

In Lower Radley there are picturesque thatched cottages with charming names . . . Baker's Close, Neats Home and Pumney.

The Vicarage, in the upper village, is one of the oldest inhabited houses in Berkshire; the timber-framed part dates from the late 13th century, there are 15th-century alterations, and much later, Victorian additions.

St. Peter's College is now a complex of buildings that include the Victorian "free perpendicular" chapel, the imposing mansion, and most interesting, the cottage. This is an almost intact example of the new houses built by the rising gentry of Queen Elizabeth's reign, such as George Stonhouse, who purchased the estate from her in 1559. An Elizabethan fireplace and other interesting features have only recently been revealed.

Much of Radley today is new, such as the St. James Estate between the railway and the church, and more recently Peachcroft Estate, built on the outskirts of Abingdon but partly in the parish. A new village hall was opened on 17th September, 1977, and is the centre for most village activities, including the Harvest Supper.

St. Peter's College, Radley, sits on a wooded slope outside the village, and looks out towards Abingdon to the south-west.

Remenham

Remenham derived its name from The Home of the Ravens. Although now showing nothing of its great antiquity, it appears in Domesday and there is an earlier reference in the Westminster Abbey Charter of 1076.

Its 1600 or so acres consist mainly of farms and woodland, sparsely populated—a reason why much of its rural character has been preserved.

The parish is contained within the massive horse-shoe bend in the Thames between Wargrave and Hurley; the three-mile section between Marsh and Hambleden Locks forming almost the entire boundary. One of the river's famous beauty spots, Temple Island, with its fascinating Greek temple, lies a mile upstream from Hambleden.

Remenham has long enjoyed a measure of distinction derived from the siting of the Henley Royal Regatta course within the stretch of the river which bounds it; the boat marquees, the several enclosures for spectators, and the judges' and marshals' accommodation are situated on the Remenham bank.

The Henley to Maidenhead road passes through Remenham. That part of it known as White Hill, extending from Henley Bridge some mile-and-a-quarter eastwards, climbing 300 feet above the river level through an avenue cut through attractive woodland, divides the parish into its north and south areas.

Near the top, and to the north, is Remenham Place. Now a residence for elderly ladies, it was, at the beginning of the century, a preparatory school, chiefly for entrants to Wellington College. Among its pupils was Capt. Oates of the ill-fated Antarctic Expedition.

It is in the mansion and surrounding estate, Park Place, lying to the south of the road, that the records show Remenham's long association with royalty and nobility.

111

In 1719 it was owned by Lord Archibald Hamilton, Lord of the Manor of Remenham, which manor was, in the reign of Henry IV, the property of the Montford family, and later of Lord Lovelace.

From 1738 until 1753 it was the residence of H.R.H. Frederick Prince of Wales. Although, not being on good terms with his son the prince's father never visited the place, the very fine cedar tree planted in the estate at that time has always been known as The King's Cedar.

A General Conway bought the estate in 1752 and in due course he made valuable additions to the property. He had built, from stones from the ruins of Reading Abbey, "The Ragged Arch" over which runs the road from Henley to Wargrave and which provides an attractive sight when viewed from the river.

He married Lady Ailesbury. Their daughter, the Hon. Mrs. Anne Seymour Damer, a gifted sculptress, executed the masks, Thames and Isis, which respectively form the upstream and downstream keystones of Henley Bridge.

In General Conway's time lavender was grown on a commercial scale, the oil being extracted and sold.

Today the mansion and 60 acres, in possession of the Hillingdon Education Authority, functions as Park Place School, an educational establishment having amenities equal to those of a public school, for 64 boys who are physically less robust than their fellows.

Worthy of note is the hamlet of Aston, situated on the bank of the river and reached by a minor road running north from the top of White Hill. Once an embarkation point for the Aston-Hambleden ferry, it is now maintained by the Thames Conservancy as a slipway for private pleasure boats. A delightful walk along the river stretches upstream to Henley.

Midway between Aston and Henley, and standing just off the river, is Remenham's St. Nicholas Church. It is on the site of an old Norman church; the apse is reputed to have been raised exactly on the original foundations.

Though relatively small, it has, behind the altar, a beautiful piece of sculpture depicting The Last Supper. It also has The Italian Arch, a pair of iron gates, made in Siena, in the form of simulated twisted rope arranged in trellis pattern and decorated with bunches of grapes. It was a gift, in 1875, from the Noble family which at that time had succeeded to Park Place.

At one time a flourishing village surrounded the church, but it is said that the entire population was wiped out by the plague *circa* 1664.

Ruscombe About half a million years ago, an ancient Thames flowed eastwards over the gravel of Sonning Golf Links to Ruscombe, where it turned north. Many Stone Age flint implements have been collected from the gravel pits of Ruscombe Hill, and the present highway through the village was the old Saxon road.

The first recorded history occurs in the foundation charter of the Cathedral of old Sarum in 1091. Among the original endowments is listed "the church of Sunning (Sonning) with the tythes and other property thereto belonging, and ten hides of land in Rothescamp (Ruscombe)."

The eastern part of the parish, known as the "Lakes", was once a marshy swamp, flooded in winter, providing perch, pike and eel in abundance for the fishermen, and withes for the baskets which were woven by industrious villagers. In 1820 the upper part of the Broadwater Stream was carried away by the Bray Cut, thus draining the lake. The land was enclosured and cultivated.

The Church of Saint James the Great, made of flint, has a long history, but the chancel is all that remains of the old structure. The nave and tower were rebuilt in 1863-9. An ancient yew tree stands outside the main door, and a patch of rough grass with a few elms is all that remains of the village green. The 400-year-old Church Cottage is said to be the original Chaplain's House, but is no longer church property. Of the same date is the shooting and fishing lodge where George I was reputed to pause for a meal when out for a day's sport from Windsor. Mr. Jack Dyer, a master thatcher, is living there today.

Portions of a mystery tunnel surrounding the parish have teased many theorists. Was it built and used by the Romans, was it a hiding-place for highwaymen, or an escape route for notable fighters in the Civil War? There is a tradition of some skirmish hereabouts, as the Register of Burials in the church records the interment of 13 soldiers between January 21st and March 22nd, 1642.

William Penn, famous as the founder of Pennsylvania and a thorough-going Quaker, lived in the parish from 1710 until his death in 1718. He used to drive through Twyford, in a coach-and-four on his way to Friends' Meetings in Reading. The house he lived in was pulled down in 1830, probably Ruscombe House, which was in the field opposite Southbury Farm. The original bakehouse and dairy buildings were finally demolished a few years

113

ago, revealing an unsuspected stairway and attic room. Legend says that this was a highwayman's hideout. Penn's name lives on in the Rural District Council Estate of Pennfields.

St. Sebastian

When the Women's Institute of St. Sebastian's compiled its Scrap Book in 1965, the introduction read: "We have no village, nor has there ever been one from which we can claim descent, unless perhaps from an early community of forest workers known as 'Broom Dashers'. These men made a living by making brooms which were sold in Reading or sent to Bristol for export. They were an isolated group of Heath dwellers who were said to be 'heathens' worshipping small china idols! The Baptists were the first to attempt regeneration. A young man from Heelas' draper story in Wokingham used to hold an occasional Sunday service."

The parish of St. Sebastian lies between Wokingham and Crowthorne and is mainly an area of woods and farms and large housing developments. The East Berkshire Golf Course saves the district from total urbanisation. The Victorian church, built by public subscription, was intended as a "Chapel of Ease" for the Broom Dashers.

The arrival of Wellington College helped to tame the wilderness of the district and gradually the Broom Dashers disappeared, crowded out by the privileged families, who built large houses bent on establishing that "gracious way of life" the Victorians enjoyed. These big houses are now turned into private schools, Ludgrove, Luckley, Oakfield, Bigshotte and Holme Grange. Ravenswood is a Village Settlement and centre for Special Education.

The visitor to the parish will find it difficult to pass two of the three inns that lie within the parish boundaries. The Crooked Billet is 153 years old, and even older the Who'd a tho't it. There is a local story about the origin of this unusual name. One day the Duke of Wellington was riding in Windsor Forest and realised that both he and his horse were very thirsty. Scouts from his party were sent ahead, down a track in the forest, now known as Nine Mile Ride, to search for liquid refreshment. They came across a timbered tavern in the forest hamlet of St. Sebastian and sent back word to the Duke. On his arrival at the tavern he is reputed to have said, "By Gad! Who would have thought it?" In February 1971 it was decided to paint a new sign for the inn. This now shows the astronauts on the moon! "Who'd a tho't it?"

Not far from the Who'd a tho't it is a section owned by the Forestry Commission known as Gorrick. Here was once a well famous for the healing power of its water, especially for those troubled with eye disorders. It is believed that Queen Elizabeth I visited the well three times. The site of the Gorrick Well is preserved as an antiquity.

Sandhurst, on the banks of the Blackwater, boasts an old settlement with a name of Saxon origin. "Hurst" meaning a "wooded eminence" and sand referring to the type of soil. A few peasant huts clustered together below the outcrop, in a sheltered dell, surrounded by moorland, where the only possible industry was the cutting of tods or turves. During the reign of Henry VIII the breeding of sheep was introduced in the area known as Sheep Rayles (now Snaprails) and slowly the population began to increase. It is said that Prince Arthur crossed the Blackwater at Yateley Mill, on his way to welcome his future bride, Catherine of Aragon, from Spain.

Forest End House, with Hart's Leap Road and Hart's Leap Close, mark the edge of Windsor Forest. George III is thought to have owned a Hunting Lodge thereabouts. The "Old Well" on Scotland's Hill, Rackstraw Farm and Sandhurst Farm are the few ancient buildings that remain unchanged. Sandhurst is almost entirely a 19th-century development and is still expanding fast.

George III attended the first army manoeuvres that took place in the rough heath-covered land towards Easthampstead, in 1792. The obvious advantage of training the army in peace-time for war led to the building of the Royal Military Academy in 1812. The building was designed by James Wyatt in an uncompromisingly austere style. He allowed only a six-columned classical portico of great height, to break the severe two-storeyed front stretching the length of the parade ground. The Military Museum and the Park, which is stocked with unusual trees such as huge Wellingtonias and Deodars, as well as azaleas and many colonial heathers introduced by retired army officers, are unfortunately no longer freely open to the public for security reasons.

Sandhurst Church was built by G. E. Street in 1853. It has a tall Surrey-style tower and a shingled spire. The east window is a lurid Victorian effort which effectively darkens the church, along with the other stained glass memorials to departed soldiers.

Edward VI in his zeal for religious unity rifled the original ancient church, of which nothing remains, of its treasures. The parish records note that the confiscation included "a summe of eytepence a year to fill two lamps with oyle for ever".

Swallowfield, a large parish of nearly 400 acres, includes the hamlet of Riseley Common, once called West Swallowfield.

Part of the Roman road from Silchester to London, now called "The Devil's Highway" or "the Banks", forms the southern boundary of the parish, and the whole district was once part of Windsor Great Forest.

The name of the village comes from "swale", an old German word meaning "rushing water"—an earlier name for the River Blackwater, one of the three rivers which flow through the parish.

Swalfelle Manor, mentioned in Domesday Book, was owned, after the Conquest, by a succession of Norman lords, but in 1353 it became Crown property.

Lord Clarendon inherited the estate in 1670, and he and Lady Clarendon greatly enlarged and improved the house and gardens, employing the famous architect Talman, an assistant to Sir Christopher Wren. The stucco ceiling of the oval vestibule, where the Clarendon arms can be seen, and the fine stone gateway, now at the entrance to the walled garden, are Talman's work. The exterior of the house is still very much as the Clarendons left it—that of a 17th-century mansion.

The estate was sold in 1719 to Thomas Pitt, often known as "Diamond Pitt", since it was from the sale of a huge diamond bought in India that he paid for the property. His grandson, William Pitt, who became Prime Minister and Lord Chatham, spent some of his holidays at Swallowfield. "Diamond" Pitt built the beautiful five-arch bridge over the River Blackwater.

Sir Henry Russell, who like Thomas Pitt had a distinguished career in India, purchased the estate in 1820, and the Russell family continued to live in the house, which had come to be known as "Swallowfield Park", until 1965. They entertained various celebrated people, including Dickens, Wilkie Collins, Thackeray, Charles Kingsley (author-Vicar at nearby Eversley), and Mary Mitford. The fame of the grounds, containing rare and beautiful trees, the gardens and glasshouses, was widespread, and the parkland was the backcloth for many and varied village festivities.

In 1965 the house, with 25 acres of land, was bought by the Mutual Households Association, and the interior extensively altered to provide apartments for about 50 retired people who have been living there since June 1967. The public rooms are on view to visitors on two afternoons each week during the summer months, as are the grounds which stretch down to the River Loddon. The daffodils and rhododendrons make a fine show, and there are examples of rare trees such as the catalpa, swamp poplar and the hickory. These, together with the ancient yew in the churchyard, and the Snake's Head Fritillaries which grow in a field near Riseley, are well worth seeing.

The Parish Church of All Saints stands on the north bank of the River Blackwater in the south-east corner of the Park, and about half a mile from the centre of Swallowfield village. This beautiful little church was built by Sir John le Despencer, Lord of the Manor, in 1256. It is believed that he built on the ruins of an earlier chapel, since parts of the church, such as the east window and the north and east doors, are older than the rest. The stone coffin below the west window is probably Sir John's. Interesting brasses on the floor near the altar include one showing Margery Letterford, who died in 1442, and another depicting Christopher Lyttcott, who died in 1554, with his wife and three children. The five bells, two of which date from 1660, were repaired in 1971.

Mary Russell Mitford, the author, loved the church, as can be seen from her writing: ". . . No village church was ever more happily placed: it is the very image of peace and humbleness inculcated within its walls. . . ." Miss Mitford moved, with her father, to the neighbouring village of Three Mile Cross in 1820, and so started her friendship with Lady Russell of Swallowfield Park, which was to endure for 34 years, and to prove such a consolation, particularly in her declining years. The last four years of her life she spent in a cottage in Swallowfield, arriving with a cartful of books at her new home, a red brick cottage (since enlarged) at Handpost, near the A33 in Riseley.

Miss Mitford had a serious accident in 1852, when out driving in the grounds of Swallowfield Park. The carriage overturned, and she was flung, with great violence, on to the hard road, sustaining severe injuries. Her spine was injured and she lost all power in her legs and left arm.

The accident was the beginning of the end; she lingered on for another two years, a helpless cripple suffering great pain. Her mental faculties were unimpaired, and this probably hastened her end. She could not rest, and within a few weeks of the accident she was receiving visitors, chief among them Lady Russell and her daughters. Charles Kingsley, who visited her often, describes her at this, the twilight of her life: ". . . I can never forget the little figure rolled up in two chairs in the little Swallowfield room, packed round with books up to the ceiling . . . with clothes on, of course, but of no recognized pattern; and somewhere out of the upper end of the heap, gleaming under a great, deep, globular brow, two such eyes as I never, perhaps, saw in any other English-woman . . . and such a tongue, for the beautiful speech which came out of that ugly (it was that) face; and the glitter and depth, too, of the eyes, like live coals. . . ."

It was to the Rev. Hugh Pearson, vicar of Sonning, that she wrote her last letter, on January 8th: ". . . I had many letters to answer, which brought on exhaustion of the brain . . . got over it through ten glasses of brandy , . . but it has left me much weaker . . . if you wish for another cheerful evening with your old friend, there is no time to be lost." Two days later she died, at five o'clock in the afternoon with Lady Russell beside her, loyal companion to the last.

So it was in 1855 Mary Mitford was buried under the elm trees behind the church she loved.

Swallowfield's most distinguished and beloved resident lies within sight and sound of a tributary of the Loddon which she loved so well.

Shaw-cum-Donnington

As you enter Newbury from the north before the road dips down into the town, you will see Donnington on your right and Shaw below on the left. The proud Castle of Donnington is reduced to a tower and gate house, but once was described by Camden as "a little but very neat castle, seated on the brow of a woody hill having a fine prospect and windows on all sides, very lightsome".

The woody hill and the fine prospect are still there . . . it is a lovely part of the county to explore, and a favourite place for picnics.

Sir Richard Abberbury, who was guardian to King Richard II, fortified and crenellated the little castle; Thomas Chaucer, son of the "father of English poetry", later owned Donnington, and Queen Elizabeth I certainly visited it in 1568. Her visit created a great furore of cleaning and repairing, and the expenses include "planking the bridge into the castle, mendinge the chamber floures, lyning the windows, washing the great leade pipes and making and repayring of the dores, making shedes for the kitchen and offices, and tables, formes and trussels".

It was no joke when the Queen decided to drop in on her more deserving subjects.

The "little but very neat castle" was destroyed in the Civil Wars, besieged by General Dalbier and held for the King by Sir John Boys in one of the longest sieges of the times. Also sadly destroyed was Donnington Priory, a Trinitarian House founded in 1360, and the hospital (1394) built "to establish a house of God for a minister and certain poor persons to pray for the King's soul and the Founder's soul".

The new Almshouses for women, called Abberbury Close, were built in 1938, but in Tudor style of architecture with tall chimneys and gay little gardens, looking much older and more mellow than they actually are.

Shaw, on the other side of the main road, also manages to preserve a proper village air, although the outskirts of Newbury are very near.

There are some delightful cottages, the Church of St. Mary, rebuilt on an ancient foundation in 1841; a village hall, some new housing estates, and a fine secondary school.

The great attraction is Shaw House, said to be the finest Elizabethan domestic architecture in the County. The manor was granted to Henry Dolman of Newbury, clothmaker, in 1557, and the lovely house completed in 1581.

Charles I stayed here just before the battle of Newbury, and near the east window of the library can be seen the mark of a shot, allegedly aimed at the King.

Shaw-cum-Donnington is a good place to wander in, and well worth a voyage of discovery.

Shefford Woodlands

This beautiful place-name exactly describes the little hamlet of Shefford Woodlands . . . it sits above the Lambourn Valley village of Great Shefford and among lovely woodlands. When hazel wood was of great value for thatching, hurdles, gardens and firewood, every farm had its own "woodlands" on higher ground, and from this the little settlement grew.

At the beginning of this century the population was 70 souls . . . today it is 79, so Shefford Woodlands is very much as it always has been. There was never a school here, the children going down the hill to Great Shefford School.

The church of St. Stephen was originally a Wesleyan Chapel, converted in 1911, and with some fine interior carving by Captain

Burmester, a large landowner of the time. There was always a water problem in the hamlet, and a tankhouse which collected rain water from the roofs was the main source of supply; until Captain Burmester sank a well at Woodlands House and allowed each household one bucket of water a day for the kettle.

There are several attractive cottages to see, and the picturesque Pheasant Inn, thatched and mainly of wood and therefore known as "the boarden house". The Little House in the centre of the village was once a baker's and grocery shop. Heathside Cottage has a delightful thatched roof, one of the two left in the village.

Shefford Woodlands has its link with an infamous crime . . . it was a local midwife who was blindfolded and taken to Littlecote to deliver a child whom she saw murdered by its father. The distraught woman had enough presence of mind to cut a piece of fabric from the bed curtain and to count the number of steps when she was taken out of the house. Her testimony led to the murderer's discovery, but, like many another 17th-century nobleman, he seemed to be above the law.

In 1904 the villagers raised money to buy a small Protestant church from Lady Craven of Ashdown, and made it into a reading room and general purposes village hall. In this small community it is mainly used by the Women's Institute.

Above Shefford Woodlands runs the old Roman road, Ermin Street, from Speen towards Cirencester. Nearly 2,000 years after it was built another great road hurries by the tiny village . . . the M4 has an intersection point here, and has greatly altered the pattern of local lanes.

Down the hill to the Lambourn Valley the visitor will find at East Shefford the fine church of St. Thomas, with the tombs of the Fettiplace family, who held lands in many North Berkshire villages in the 15th century. There is a fine alabaster monument to Thomas Fettiplace, Sheriff of Berkshire in 1435, and his wife Beatrice.

The Church of St. Mary's at Great Shefford has some good Transitional Norman architecture, and an unusual round tower in flint stone.

At the Manor farmhouse nearby is a secret room where popular belief claims that Charles I sheltered during the Civil Wars.

Shinfield lies three miles south of Reading and is bounded by the River Loddon to the south and east, Grazeley to the west, and Spencers Wood to the south. The earliest settlement was in Saxon times, Domesday Book stating that the King held "Selingfelde in demesne". The Loddon provided drinking water, valuable fisheries and power for a mill.

William the Conqueror gave the Manors of Shinfield and Swallowfield to William FitzOsbern, Lord of Breteuil in Normandy and Earl of Hereford, who founded St. Mary's Church about 1070. A list of Vicars, inside the church, goes back to 1280. The advowson of the church was granted in 1289 to the Bishop of Hereford, and remains with the Dean and Chapter of Hereford to this day. In 1312 Edward II and the Bishop of Hereford were shooting deer in the Shinfield part of Windsor Forest, and the Bishop asked the King for assistance in rebuilding his cathedral. Later the Bishop made such a good shot at a deer that Edward agreed to give him the tithes of Shinfield and Swallowfield.

Elizabeth of York, mother of Henry VIII and Lady of the Manor of Shinfield, caused the south aisle to be built in 1475. Edward Martyn, who had been bailiff of the Royal Manor of Shinfield, was granted custody of the manor by the Queen for his own use. In 1596 he built the Martyn Chapel to the south of the chancel. Though extensively modernized, the chapel still retains its waggonhead ceiling buttoned with Tudor rosettes.

The old Manor House, probably dating from the 16th century was on the main Shinfield Road. In 1792, when repairs were done to a chimney, a Cartulary (a book in which were made copies of deeds of properties relating to Reading Abbey) was found in a blocked-up room. Probably hidden at the time of the dissolution of the Abbey in 1537, it is now in the British Museum.

An extract from *The Wonders of the Universe*, 1727, reads:

". . . . My Lord Cromwell, after his success at Dorchester, did bring his forces to Caversham to cross the river, but learning that bodies of Royalists were forming in Reading and in the country beyond, he did dispatch his troops to engage them— which troops did persue them to Shinfield and beyond—a body of the enemy having taken refuge in the Parish Church. Cannon were brought up and used, the tower being reduced. . . ."

(circa 1644)

By 1664 the tower had been restored and three of the six bells installed to celebrate the restoration of the monarchy.

In an extensive restoration of the church carried out in 1855 by Sir George Gilbert Scott, the chancel was extended and a tiled floor laid. The brasses in the floor were probably not removed at this time, and in 1936 a subsidence near the font revealed, under the tiles, the Mitford brass. This commemorates the parents of Mary Mitford, who lived at Three Mile Cross, 1820 to 1850, and who described life in Shinfield in the classic, *Our Village*.

In 1707 Richard Piggott, a Shinfield boy who became a wealthy cutler in London, built and endowed a school for 20 poor boys, to be educated up to 12 years of age. They were given new clothes every Founder's Day, and later apprenticed. The will of the Revd. G. Fields provided education for six more boys, and 6d., a bun and a glass of wine to each boy on Founder's Day, as well as a clock to strike the quarters "like the one at Brighton".

Piggott's school, with clock, on the edge of School Green, has been in use ever since its foundation, though now housing the infants only. In 1968 a well-designed Junior School was built nearby.

As a memorial to those killed in the war and as a thanksgiving for peace, the Shinfield Recreation and Sports Association decided, in 1947, to lease a field for 99 years from the National Institute for Research in Dairying, for use as a recreational field. Each Spring Bank Holiday Monday a carnival is held. The proceeds go towards upkeep of the field which provides tennis courts, cricket and football pitches, and a children's corner.

The Dairying Research Institute bought the manor, formerly the old rectory next to the church, in 1920. An old cedar tree in the manor grounds is known as Katherine's Tree. Legend has it that it was planted by Katherine of Aragon, given the manors of Shinfield and Swallowfield by Henry VIII. A national cattle breeding centre was recently established nearby.

In April 1951 a small group of people representing the Parish and Free Churches met to discuss the possibility of forming an Eisteddfod, the objects being to participate in the Festival of Britain, encourage the arts, and foster a friendly competitive local spirit. This Eisteddfod, now the Shinfield Festival, began in a very small way, but has proved so successful that every year sees a greater interest and increase of entries, particularly in the children's and drama sections.

The land acquired soon after the turn of the century by Reading College, now the University, for its agricultural students, is still in use, and this helps Shinfield to keep its farming character.

However, land on the edge of the village is being developed and a large site is occupied by the new Shire Hall and Meteorological Office Weather Centre.

Shrivenham One of the most westerly villages of old Berkshire, Shrivenham is a fine open place with much to interest the visitors. It has a wide, tree-lined main street, with many lovely thatched cottages, and is proud to have its own local thatcher, Mr. Auger.

Its population is approximately 2,900, it has a hotel, the Barrington Arms, and two public houses, the Prince of Wales and the Crown.

Shopping facilities are good, and one of the finest village halls in the county, the Memorial Hall, was presented by Charlotte, Countess Barrington, and opened by Princess Beatrice in 1925.

Beside the hall is the recreation ground, with football and cricket pitches, tennis courts and a new bowling green up to competition standards.

The ancient Manor of Becket, once held by the Count of Evreux, then by King John, and latterly the Barrington family, is now the Royal College of Military Science. The grounds are open to the public, and there are beautiful walks through snowdrop-covered woods, and a lake with a great duck population.

Another delightful walk is from Shrivenham Church via Pennyhooks Farm to Watchfield.

The original parts of the parish church are 12th century with 17th-century additions. Henry I granted the church to the Abbey of Cirencester, and the 17th-century buildings were given by Sir Henry Marten of Longworth at a cost of £4,000. This same benefactor also built the ten almshouses in 1642, and today they are still inhabited.

Sir Henry Marten's signature appears on the death warrant of Charles I, and bitter fighting during the Civil Wars took place around Shrivenham and nearby Faringdon.

Shrivenham is well worth a visit, charming to look at, and with a history going back to Roman times . . . 24 coins of the reign of Allectus (A.D. 293–296) were discovered in an old well in 1905.

The first written records of this ancient place appear in the Domesday Survey of 1085.

Silchester was a British city before the Romans came, deriving its name of Calleva Atrebatum from the Atrebates, whose kings once ruled much of southern England. Calleva means the "Woodland Town", built amongst the woods of which Pamber Forest is a remnant, and the site was chosen because of its height (300 feet above sea level), its easily defended position, and its abundant water supply.

The remains of the Roman wall, 1½ miles round, mark the outline of the city, which lies buried under the fields of Manor Farm. Excavated between 1864 and 1892, many of the treasures of Calleva are displayed in the Silchester Collection at Reading Museum, while replicas can be seen in a small museum in the village.

Accurate models were made of the Forum, the streets, squares and courtyards, before the excavations were filled in and the pasturelands restored, and now, leaning over a gate to watch the cattle and pigs, it is hard to imagine the ancient, bustling city with the trundle of cart-wheels, the shouting of traders selling their wares, the shrill laughter of the children playing in the congested colourful streets.

From gateways in the city wall, Roman roads led to Old Sarum, Winchester, London and the north. Inside the walls were found the ruins of a tiny building which is believed to be the oldest Christian church in England.

The present church of St. Mary the Virgin, standing near the site of the East Gate, was begun in the reign of King John. It was improved by succeeding Lords of the Manor, and carefully and skilfully restored in Victorian times. The chancel screen and the stained glass from the windows were hidden from Cromwell's Ironsides, and though the screen was eventually replaced in the church, the ancient glass is still missing. It was hidden so successfully that no one has been able to find it, and the people of Silchester still hope that, one day, a building worker or landscape gardener may uncover its hiding place.

The medieval cottages became deserted after the Black Death, leaving the church and Manor Farm isolated from the present centre of population, which is expanding rapidly, close to Silchester Common.

The first Duke of Wellington bought the Manor of Silchester because it belonged to his wife's family, the Longfords, and because it bordered his estate of Stratfield Saye. The present Duke is Lord of the Manor still, though the management of Silchester Common has been handed over to the Rural District Council.

Amongst the treasures excavated during the time of the second Duke was the Silchester Eagle, believed to be part of a Roman legionary standard. Also in Reading Museum is a little horse, probably designed as the handle of a mug or beaker, and resembling in style the White Horse which is cut out of the chalk hillside above Uffington.

Although Silchester is still mostly farm land, it is only eight miles from Basingstoke and twelve from Reading, between the M3 and M4 motorways.

At the time of writing, it has one general store cum post office, one public house, and an hotel. Opposite the playing field is the village hall, focal point of most village activities, and on the other two corners of the Common stand the Methodist Chapel and the Church of England Primary School.

Many motorists stop at a gap in the hedge where they can see the Silchester House clock, built by the late Mr. T. M. Hartley. Five carved wooden figures stand below the clock face—Father Time, who strikes the hours, and four people in colourful Bavarian costume, whose hammers chime the quarter bells.

Many new houses have been built in this neighbourhood, but the surrounding countryside is still supremely peaceful, sleeping as it has done those many centuries since the death of the once-thriving "Woodland Town".

THAMES, NEAR SONNING

Sonning

Turn off the busy A4 down Sonning Lane, and at once you sense the magic . . . whether it's the green tunnel of summer trees, the glowing tints of autumn, arching bare branches or glittering frost of winter, the peace is there.

Perhaps Dick Turpin felt the same sudden lightness of heart when, after a "hold-up" on the Bath Road, he galloped down the lane heading for his aunt's cottage. Tradition has it that, reaching the village, off he leapt (well-trained Black Bess making her way to the underground stable below the cottage) and raced through the churchyard, over the bridge into Oxfordshire. There he'd lie-up till the hue and cry had died down and he could join Bess. The cottage in time became The Dog, one of many inns in Sonning; it is now, with its neighbour, a private house called, of course, Turpins.

It is difficult to realize today, wandering around this small, peaceful village, that a thousand years ago it was the nerve centre of one of the largest parishes in Wessex, stretching from Sonning Common to Sandhurst. It boasted, in the 10th and 11th centuries, its own Saxon Bishops, three of whom became Archbishops of Canterbury; and from the 11th to 16th century the Bishops and Deans of Salisbury regularly visited their own vast residences here. This enormous estate was handed over to the Church in the 7th century, and was very much on the map when Reading was but a huddle of huts hugging the banks of the Kennet. Sonning's importance declined because it was not a good administrative centre for such a vast diocese; later there was the growth and rivalry of Reading Abbey.

Domesday Book records "Osmund Bishop of Sarisberie holds Soninges in demesne, in right of his Bishopric". The Bishops' rambling palace lay alongside the church, looking on to the river and the water meadows beyond. Nothing now remains of ". . . the fair olde house of stone by the Tamise ripe", as described by Leland in 1543, except grassy mounds and a stone-lined underground ice-house. Excavations carried out in 1914 showed that increasingly fine houses had been built on top of each other through the centuries. King John reputedly stayed there before signing the Magna Carta at Runnymede; and in the bleak winter of 1399 Isabella, child-wife of deposed Richard II, spent anxious and lonely months there under the protection of Richard's Bishop Confessor. Little wonder that her unhappy ghost is said to haunt the winding woodland walks by the river.

In 1574 the manor of Sonning was given to the Crown, later passing to private families, Barker and Rich chief among them. Another ghostly visitor, as the church clock strikes midnight, is a willowy Miss Rich, who allegedly floats over the ancient flint wall in Sonning Lane.

Beautiful St. Andrew's Church, much restored in 1852 by the perhaps over zealous Victorians, has interesting brasses and monuments; and if walls could talk, what tales they'd have to tell! One Vicar had a habit of striding through the village with bared sword; another in the 1570's displeased his wardens by putting a new seat for his wife ". . . in an unmeet place", and allowing his cattle to run wild in the graveyard. Grave-robbing was prevalent in the last century, the bodies being sold to unscrupulous doctors for research. One such medical gentleman from Reading was in the habit of dining with Sonning's Vicar while his confederates were at work just over the wall!

Leland reported that ". . . there is an olde Chapelle at the Est end of the Church of St. Sarik whither of late tyme resorted in pilgrimage many folkes for the disease of madness. . . ." The chapel is no more, though traces of its foundations were found when grave-digging some years back. "Saric's" identity remains a mystery, though he may have been Sigeric, a much-loved Saxon Bishop of Sonning.

The Bull Inn, next to, and still belonging to the church, has from early times figured largely in village affairs. It may well have originated as a guest-house for the pilgrims who flocked to St. Saric's, hoping for miracle cures. At the time of the Bishop or Dean's "Visitation" there was always a great dinner there—His Grace, the Squire and the gentry upstairs, and the villagers down below. On both levels food and drink flowed in abundance and there was much merry-making.

The White Hart Hotel may have originated as the home of "Elias the Ferryman" mentioned in a deed of 1100. A ferry, then wooden and later brick bridges have been near it since very early times. The following, from *Lays of a Lazy Minstrel,* still applies as much as when it first appeared in *Punch* early this century:

"Let's land at the lawn of the cheery White Hart
Now gay with the glamour of June;
For here we can lunch to the music of trees
In sight of the swift river running.
Offcuts of cold beef and a pure Cheddar cheese,
And a tankard of bitter, at Sonning."

The Thames is islanded through Sonning, and the weir plays an important part in flood control. The rare Loddon Lily grows in the woods by the lock, itself famous for its flower garden which has many times earned the coveted "garden award". Sonning used to be the centre of operations of Thames Navigation. Here lived the General Surveyor, and under his personal supervision was carried out constructive works from Lechlade to Staines, including the erection of pound-locks to replace the old flash-locks. A large, heavily laden barge needed the combined efforts of 50 to 80 men to negotiate it up through a flash-lock, and these "scuffle-hunters" were the terror of the neighbourhood. In 1773 wages of men making the towpath were 1s. 6d. per day; when working in the water, gin was provided!

The mill, rebuilt many times and operating its own fleet of barges, ceased to work, for the first time since Saxon days, in 1969. It is now converted into a theatre.

Behind the ancient Deanery wall is a fine house designed by Lutyens in 1899, standing just above the site of the old Deanery House, which fell into decay in the early 19th century. The beautiful gardens are occasionally open to the public.

Until the Great War, Sonning was an extremely active, self-sufficient village. River traffic was frequent and a small boat-building yard lay opposite the White Hart bank; osiers grew in Sonning Eye, providing a flourishing basket-making business; four farms gave employment to many; the High Street was lined with shops . . . grocers, a butcher's shop with its own slaughter-house; tailor, newsagent and sweet shop, post office and bakery. Residents to this day recall the glorious odour at lunchtime on a Sunday morning as many people, after church, collected their joints cooked for them at 1d. a time at the bakery, and carried them home steaming and succulent under a white cloth!

A flourishing coach-building works in Thames Street turned out superb examples of dedicated craftsmanship. A resident still tells of his feeling of pride as he completed the 16th coat of paint on one such vehicle, under the eagle eye of Mr. Cox. Next to this was the village dairy. Further along the road is "The Acre", where Holman Hunt painted *The Light of the World*.

The fields of Reading University Farm stretch down to the river. It was in Straighthanger Field, a few years back, that a Neolithic enclosure was excavated, and a remarkably fine pair of bronze bangles found.

Back to Pearson Road, named after Canon Hugh Pearson, beloved Vicar here from 1841 to 1882. Rambling Sonningdene, opposite the village hall, was once the summer retreat of Whig-wit Revd. Sydney Smith; the most treasured possession at The Old Cottage is a dainty, faded brocade shoe, blocked up in a wall for some 400 years; The Grove, facing down the High Street, was temporary "prison" for French Admiral Villeneuve (thanks to Nelson), and weekend retreat for General Eisenhower in a later war.

Houses now line Pound Lane, but villagers remember when there were only hop fields, meadows, and the Pound for straying cattle.

And so up Sonning Lane again. Away to the right is Holme Park, the mansion built by the Palmers in 1800, now housing Reading Blue Coat School.

Sonning boasts its own Fire Station, manned by volunteers, and a thriving Working Men's Club. The "Best-kept Village" plaque has often graced the "hall".

The village is anxious to preserve its identity, and lives in the present as well as treasuring its past. In the Middle Ages it was a place of pilgrimage, and today, despite the traffic, modern pilgrims can still enjoy the peace and beauty of its ancient streets and riverside walks.

Sparsholt

A steeply descending road from the Downs between Wantage and Ashbury brings one to the pretty village of Sparsholt. The quiet of the Vale of the White Horse lies all around, the old cottages and houses are attractively grouped, there are many fine trees, and relatively little infilling of modern housing.

The glory of Sparsholt is the Holy Rood Church, large for such a small village: there are two interesting monumental brasses, one of a churchman under a canopy and another showing a gowned and bearded member of the Fettiplace family who was a dwarf.

On the north wall of the chancel, cut into a large stone, is the design for the medieval game of Nine Men's Morris, rare in any place today. In Shakespeare's *Midsummer Night's Dream* there is a notable reference to the game, and similar stones in the castles of Norwich, Scarborough and Dover indicate that it was played by men-at-arms in their leisure hours. Cut in the benches of the cloisters at Salisbury and Gloucester it would appear that schoolboys also enjoyed the game.

Nine Men's Morris was probably a simple form of medieval chess, played on a flat stone, so the wall stone at Sparsholt must have lain flat before it was built into the wall in the first half of the 14th century.

Another great attraction to draw visitors to Holy Rood Church are the Sparsholt effigies, carved wooden figures of Sir Robert Achard, who died in 1353, and his two wives, Joanna and Agnes. Out of 96 medieval wooden effigies in England today, only six are in Berkshire, and three of these can be seen at Sparsholt.

Sir Robert lies on a wooden table in the middle of the transept floor, somewhat faded and damaged over the centuries; Agnes and Joanna are placed in recesses in the wall and have fared a little better, though Agnes has lost an arm and some of her supporting nuns and angels are somewhat the worse for wear. Of great interest to antiquarians, the Sparsholt effigies, in the full glory of their original gilding and brilliant paint, must have been a truly splendid sight in their chantry.

129

We are indebted for this information to the late A. G. Shireff, whose work for Murray's *Berkshire Architectural Guide* is of great value.

Speen On the outskirts of Newbury, and an older village than the invading market town, Speen was once a flourishing settlement on the Roman road from Silchester to Cirencester. It bravely preserves its village atmosphere despite the encroaching urban development and the constant traffic of the A4, Bath Road.

The beautiful church of St. Mary the Virgin retains much of the 13th-century fabric, despite Victorian restoration, the 600-year-old North Chapel window being its chief treasure. Medieval stained glass is set in a lovely carved tracery, and the nave is supported by Purbeck stone columns of great beauty.

Look for two fine altar tombs east of the chancel . . . the armoured effigy of John Baptiste Castillion (1598), who received the Manor of Speen from Queen Elizabeth I in return for "faithful service in her dangers"; and a beautifully carved effigy of Dame Elizabeth Castillion (1603), daughter-in-law of John, showing a gown and farthingale and a most interesting horned headdress.

In a little lane leading to the church you will find Our Lady Well, where the water allegedly has healing and mystic powers. One of Speen's residents claims to have seen an apparition by the well.

At Speen Hill the Cavaliers and Roundheads fought during the Civil Wars, this part of Berkshire being a centre of strife for long periods. Clustered round the church are several well-preserved Regency houses, and a beautiful 400-year-old farmhouse and barn which has been carefully restored. The Hare and Hounds Inn is another fine old building.

There is a war memorial at Speen, a Victorian village hall built in 1886, an old pound, and Speen Church House, which has been made into a home for the aged.

Spencers Wood If you make the journey from St. Giles Church in Southampton Street, Reading, and travel due south for four miles, you arrive at Milestone Cottage in the centre of Spencers Wood village. The milestone still stands outside the cottage, on which site, many years ago, stood the Four Mile Inn—a welcome spot, no doubt, for thirsty villagers after the long walk back from morning service at St. Giles's. Behind the cottage, where the Congregational Manse now stands, was the Nonconformist Chapel built in 1837.

Most of the houses in the village were built from bricks made in the local brick kiln, in use till early 1900, using clay dug from pits in the nearby common.

As you approach the village there is, on the brow of the hill, the lovely Queen Anne period Hill House, and the hawthorn bush at the driveway entrance, mentioned by Miss Mary Mitford in her classic *Our Village*: "We are now on the very brow of the eminence close to the Hill House and its beautiful gardens. On the outer edge of the paling, hanging over the bank that skirts the road, is an old thorn—such a thorn! The long sprays covered with snowy blossom, so graceful, so elegant, so lightsome, and yet so rich! . . ."

The nearby butcher's shop was formerly the Cricketers' Arms. On the wall in the shop is a framed letter dated 1888, sent by Queen Victoria from Osborne House, Isle of Wight. It is an order for 36 lb. of sirloin from a bullock purchased from Shaw Farm, Windsor—beef at that time weighing in at about 9d. per lb.!

On land behind the shop are the remains of the school for which pupils paid one penny per day.

The Hunter family, from nearby Beech Hill, donated land and money for the building of the nearby Anglican Church in 1908, to the east of which an Elizabethan cottage now does duty as a doctor's surgery. A "lock-up" that used to stand on adjacent land was used for local miscreants, and also as an overnight stop for prisoners who had been marched from Basingstoke, presumably to appear at Reading Court next day.

An attractive feature of the village is the driveway of Wellingtonia trees which were planted during the lifetime of the first Duke of Wellington. At the end of the avenue is the site of a former country mansion called "Stanbury", which unfortunately had to be demolished after the last war. The trees have seen many changes; first as shelter for Nissen huts for soldiers, then for German P.o.W.'s, and lastly for local citizens who would otherwise have been homeless. Fortunately the huts were cleared away and the avenue restored to its former glory. Opposite the driveway a stately oak tree commemorates the diamond jubilee of Queen Victoria.

A wheelwright's shop opposite probably made wheels for the carriages built by Messrs. Hewitt and Beacon, situated at the far end of the village on the site now occupied by Double's Garage.

In the late 1890's Mr. Double, Senior, opened a blacksmith's shop, being joined later by his two sons, all of whom held the country's championship in their trade. At the time there was sufficient employment for four men at Spencers Wood forge, and for two men at Grazeley. It was a common sight, even until 1964, to see horses waiting outside the shop, while others inside were being shod, and there were always many interested spectators of all ages. The late Mr. C. Double retired in 1964, and the forge is now a light engineering factory.

Messrs. Webb had a saddlers' shop opposite the village pond, and nearby stands the shed built to house the first horse bus which ran from Reading to Riseley. Later the shed was the home of the village fire engine.

Many changes have been made in Spencers Wood since the last war; former apple orchards are now modern housing estates; where once horse-drawn coaches made their leisurely way to the southern ports, heavy traffic now speeds down the A33 for all roads to the coast.

But the village still keeps some of its individuality, not least being the mile and a half road through the village, pleasantly shaded by alternate planting of acacia, pine and beech trees.

Stanford Dingley,

one of Berkshire's most beautiful villages, has a lovely setting in the valley of the Pang. It is as attractive as its name, the first part of which it owes to William de Standford, in 1224 Lord of the Manor, and the second to Richard Dyneley, mentioned in 1428 as the son of William Dyneley, Esquire, of the Bodyguard to Henry VI.

Other notable sons of the village were Thomas Teasdale, who made a fortune in the parish as a clothier, and later founded Pembroke College, Oxford. John Lyford, Citizen and Merchant Taylor of London, lord of the very ancient manor of Rushdens in the village, whose family also distinguished themselves as weavers and merchants in the clothing trade. Dr. Richard Valpy, Headmaster of Reading School from 1781, who had the Stanley Dingley advowson, and made his brother rector. Three other Valpys also served the parish. Another village worthy, Thomas Smith, became a factor to the Turkey merchants, died in Constantinople in 1623 leaving £20 to purchase a piece of land towards the maintenance of the church.

The village can be justly proud of its old buildings, its mill was first mentioned in the Domesday Book. It has a 15th-century coaching inn, several scheduled buildings, and numerous attractive houses and cottages. Two outstanding are the Old Rectory, a splendid Georgian house of mellow red brick, with attractive dormer windows, and a moulded wooden doorcase of Doric design; and the Garden House of a slightly later period.

The charming and picturesque church, screened by Spanish chestnut trees, has a wealth of interest. Certainly a Saxon church was standing here before the Conquest. The present form is largely the result of building about 1200; but parts of the original masonry are contained in the walls at the west end of the Nave. The font is plain, probably Norman, the roof is finely timbered, and a splendid 13th-century door, with contemporary ironwork, is plainly part of the original scheme. Restoration work in 1870 revealed wall paintings and some frescoes, which date from the 13th century. The very high walls of the Nave display a large scheme of murals; St. Christopher is depicted on the north-west wall. Some of the paintings are sadly faded, but conventional scrolls of vines can be seen and on the west side a complete figure represents St. Edmund. Opposite is the face of a corresponding figure, who may be another notable saint, St. Thomas à Becket. Built into the north side of the chancel arch are some fine 14th-century encaustic tiles depicting the Star of David, the Lamb of God, the mask of a lion and two chalices. Another treasure is the wooden relief carving of the Royal Arms of William and Mary, a rarity indeed. There are three good brasses, a particularly good one being that of Margaret Dyneley, 1444.

The church is dedicated to St. Denys. Few churches in England bear his name. Legend has it that he was martyred in Paris during the 3rd century by beheading. He is said to have picked up his severed head, and walked away with it. Where he put it down he was buried and a church built to St. Denys. He has always been portrayed decapitated in medieval art, his head in his hands, and is indeed so represented on the lectern in Stanford Dingley church.

Throughout the ages industries have thrived in Stanford Dingley. Alongside the brick and weatherboard mill (mentioned in Domesday records) was the tannery, one of the oldest industries in Berkshire, based originally on ample supplies of oak bark. The former smithy, adjacent to its minute cottage, can be found in the centre of the village opposite the Bull Inn. More recently there was a bottle factory near the bridge, and its products are occasionally found in the gardens close by.

No self-respecting English village is without at least one ancient inn. Stanford Dingley can boast of two splendid ones. The Bull, an old 15th-century coaching inn with a wealth of old beams, is famous locally for the game played there—"Ring the Bull"—the object being to swing a ring suspended from the ceiling by a cord on to a horn; certainly a game of some antiquity. The Boot Inn, though not so old, is reputedly haunted by a man who hanged himself in its orchard. Doors are said to close mysteriously at times; and speaking of ghosts—the Old Rectory is said to have one, and a shrouded woman is said to walk in Jennets Wood at midnight.

Stanford-in-the-Vale

A stone ford over the little River Ock explains the first part of this delightful village name, and the Vale is that plain in the north above which the White Horse prances. Just off the A417, six miles from Wantage and four from Faringdon, this attractive place, built around two village greens, has a present population of about 2,000.

The lovely church of St. Denys, beside one of the greens, has an 80-feet-high tower, and is mainly of Early English and Decorated Architecture. The original bells have been replaced by the eight-bell peal from the disused church of St. Peter-in-the-East, Oxford, and rang out over Stanford for the first time in 1970, after having been silent since 1944.

The visitor to the church will find much of interest . . . the south porch was built in 1472 to commemorate the marriage of Anne Neville, daughter of Warwick the Kingmaker, to Richard, Duke of Gloucester, afterwards Richard III.

Another link with the royal house of York is that Jane Colyns, of Stanford-in-the-Vale, was nursemaid to Prince Edward, born in 1473 to Richard of Gloucester and his wife Anne. This delicate child lived only a few years. For her services Jane was paid 100 shillings a year.

Enthusiasts of monumental brasses will find an interesting floor brass of Roger Campdene, Rector of the parish, a half figure in priest's robes, with four corner emblems of the Evangelists, and dated 1398.

On the south wall is a piscina surmounted by a beautifully carved reliquary; tradition has it that a finger of St. Denys was preserved here, probably lent by the Benedictine monks of Abingdon Abbey.

For the amateur of gravestones there is an interesting one carved with a frying pan . . . the resting place of a gypsy woman who died while cooking. Another is inscribed to a gypsy with the unusual name of Gravellene, and a High Sheriff of Berkshire, one Captain Hatt, who fought at Culloden Moor in 1746, is also buried at Stanford-in-the-Vale.

The churchyard has a ghost, or grey lady recently seen flitting about at night, but nobody knows who she is or why she flits.

The Vicarage is large and Victorian, and the living includes the villages of Goosey and Hatford, and is the gift of the Dean and Chapter of Westminster.

One of the little settlement's noteworthy Vicars was Christopher Wordsworth (1850–1869), a nephew of the poet, and creator of many hymns, including "Gracious Spirit, Holy Ghost".

Stanford-in-the-Vale has some beautiful houses in the old centre of the village. A row of lovely cottages beside Church Green include Vine Cottages, much photographed, and with a fire-mark of the Royal Exchange Insurance Company, 1786.

The Manor House, built in 1618 on an older foundation, has some fine panelling and a Jacobean staircase. The Norman owner of the Manor was Henry de Ferrers; later the well-known Fettiplace family acquired it, and it subsequently passed on to the Knollys clan, Earls of Banbury, one of whom built the present house.

An imposing early 17th-century house called Penstone's Farm was one of Cromwell's many stopping places in the Civil Wars.

The beautiful Queen Anne Rectory House has a Tudor annexe, and once contained a Tudor charcoal burner which is now stored in the cellar of the main house.

Besides all these survivals of the historic past, Stanford-in-the-Vale has a flourishing modern community, with extensive new housing, an excellent primary school catering for children from Goosey, Hatford and Challow Station as well as the local young. It is a village with many thriving social clubs, a post office, several shops, a supermarket, a woodyard, nurseries, an undertaker and builder; and, hallmark of the times, a do-it-yourself shop.

Steventon

Mention Steventon to anyone in the north of Berkshire and they will think of the village green . . . probably the finest in the county, set about with ancient houses and noble chestnuts, and bisected from east to west by the raised Causeway. Along this stone pathway the feet of monks, villagers and travellers have passed for centuries, going westward to the Downs and the great Sheep Fair at Ilsley, and east towards the Abbey of Abingdon, centre of learning and religion until the mid-16th century.

The A34 bypass was completed in November 1977, thus relieving Steventon of the heavy traffic which had plagued it for so long.

For the visitor on foot the village is an architectural delight. Start at the parish church of St. Michael, a lovely village church with beautiful timbered roof, and notice the Manor Farm opposite. This is a good square Queen Anne house, with a wonderful barn raised on arches above flood level. Nearby the partly 16th-century Mill House has been carefully restored, and beside it the millstream cascades over a miniature waterfall.

The Priory and Priory Cottage date from 1462, and surround a courtyard. This beautiful house is National Trust property, and the Great Hall, dated about 1500, contains a fine hammerbeam roof and is open to the public on Wednesday afternoons.

At the railway level crossing stands one of the oldest houses in the village (No. 89) and nearby is Cruck House, beautifully preserved from the 14th century, in which no original feature is dated later than 1350.

Steventon is rich in timber and plaster houses, and there are several beautifully restored on the east side of the Causeway.

B.R. Western region trains rush through Steventon, but they no longer stop . . . the stone-built station and cottages have been partly demolished. The materials that built the railway were brought by the Wilts. and Berks. Canal, which connected the Thames with the Kennet and the Avon. Now the canal, too, has gone, and very little trace of it remains.

The village has a great many new houses on its outskirts and along the Hanney Road; and on the Green a very handsome village hall, much used by the greatly enlarged population. A Fair visits Steventon for several days annually, cricket is enthusiastically played on the Green, and a great range of clubs and societies hold social gatherings in the hall.

Steventon has a long and honourable past, an active and interesting present, and a hopeful future.

Stockcross

Not far from Newbury on the north of the A4, Bath Road, you will find the little village of Stockcross. The main road through the settlement is that old Roman highway, Ermin Street, but the village itself is by comparison new . . . it was largely built in the early 19th century as a model village.

Benham House, a fine Georgian House built in 1775 under the direction of Henry Holland, was the home of the Sutton family until the 1939–45 war; and it was Sir Richard Sutton who in 1903 built much of the village as it looks today.

The pretty little Tudor-style cottages were planned to give an overall "old world" look to Stockcross, and most of them are tenanted by retired employees of the estate.

When the Suttons moved out, the big house was temporarily in the hands of American Servicemen.

The old school, built in 1832, was demolished in 1971. In Victorian days the estate children paid one penny a week to master the three R's, and this meagre offering formed part of the head teacher's salary.

Stockcross was very much a self-contained village . . . the men worked on the estate, in the brick kiln, at the coaching stables by the Bath Road, and at Burton's smithy. There was a busy estate laundry where, until recently, one could see the huge copper and massive ironing tables. It is recorded that Percy Carpenter was an expert with the goffering iron! In the present post office garden was the aptly name Buster Bune's Bakehouse.

There are several public houses . . . the Rising Sun, the Cricketers' Inn, and the Nag's Head, now renamed the Lord Lyon, after a Derby winner of 1866 . . . owned, of course, by Sir Richard Sutton.

St. John's Church, 1839, but built in the Early English style, is worth a visit. The stained glass windows, the fine alabaster reredos and the superb chancel screen, were all designed by Sir Ninian Comper. There is an attractive Lady Chapel dedicated as a war memorial to the men who died in the first World War.

Stockcross has a good village hall, known as Sutton Hall, used for all the recreations of the village, and as a memorial to Mrs. Pilkington of Folly Lodge, Stockcross has a village seat surrounded by flowering trees.

Here is a tiny corner of Berkshire with an atmosphere all its own, and a very peaceful air of going steadfastly about its own business.

Streatley

In the Goring Gap between the River Thames and the Downs lies the lovely village of Streatley, favourite riverside port of call for innumerable small boats and weekend sightseers. The Swan Inn, plushy and popular, lies along the towpath beside the weir, gay with flowers, ducks, and swans. Above it the road bridge leads over to Goring and Oxfordshire.

The old wooden bridge with toll-gate for carts, toll-house and pedestrian gate was replaced in 1926.

About 900 people live in Streatley, in handsome old houses and cottages grouped around the bridge and church, and some excellent modern houses on the A329, which cuts through the village below the well-wooded downs.

In the early part of this century the brewing family of Morrell owned three-quarters of Streatley, in land, woods and farms. A beautiful William and Mary house in the High Street was their home.

Another fine house of the same period is the residence of a local doctor, and an Elizabethan farmhouse, once Place Manor Farm, is supposed to be haunted by a lady in white!

The Norman church of St. Mary is attractively set among trees behind the Swan Inn and off the main road; it was extensively restored in Victorian times.

Higher up on the A329 is the old Bull Inn, a good black and white building of considerable charm, and once a coaching inn for the Royal Mail coach to Oxford.

The land around Streatley rises steeply on both sides of the river, with fine views and noble trees . . . its natural setting is as beautiful as any in Berkshire, and on a fine sunny day admiring visitors converge on it from all corners of the world.

Sulham & Tidmarsh

Many years before the present villages of Sulham and Tidmarsh were formed, the Romans built a fine straight road that ran through Pangbourne to the Bath Road just outside Theale. This old road forded the River Pang by Longbridge Cottage in Tidmarsh, passed the old house of Bere Sizes (reputed to belong to Reading Abbey), and ran across to Sulham. Then it went down the lane, past the church to Nunhide and out to the Bath Road.

Twentieth-century road-builders have constructed the M4 Motorway which also crosses both villages, and it has to be seen what effect this will have on the community.

The village of Sulham lies under a splendid ridge of beech trees, and boasts four fine old houses, and a number of interesting period cottages which have nearly all been modernized, the post office and the village school both having closed within the past seven years.

The 13th-century St. Nicholas' Church was pulled down in 1832, but rebuilt by the Rev. John Wilder, the design being influenced by a visit he had made to Italy. The semi-circular marble font was built in 1733, and the church plate is 17th and 18th century.

The Wilder family were Lords of the Manor, and Rectors of the village since 1785. About three-quarters of a mile from the village lies Purley Hall, where Warren Hastings lived whilst awaiting his trial.

Farming and forestry are the main occupations; there is also a riding stable and a milk distribution centre.

Nunhide farmhouse is very old, and has some interesting panelling and brick wine cellars, while Sulham farmhouse has medieval wall paintings.

In Tidmarsh, the church of St. Lawrence is of Norman origin, with a unique south door, and the sculptured Norman font was found buried in the churchyard a century ago. The Rector also serves the neighbouring village of Sulham.

The 12th-century Greyhound Inn is of cruck construction with timber framing, and the thatch sweeps almost to the ground at the rear. It has served as an inn since 1625.

The village shop was, until 20 years ago, also the bakery, the Mill House is now used partly as an antique shop, and although the Forge, as such, has closed, welding is sometimes carried out there.

History relates that in 1239 there was a vineyard in Tidmarsh, perhaps belonging to the monks of Reading Abbey, who owned a house nearby.

Occupations carried on in the village are very varied; one man breeds greyhounds; the police rescue kennels are at Tidmarsh Manor; there is a breeze block manufactory, several farms including a beef smallholding, and an egg-producing unit.

The whole area is well served with public footpaths; the Village Hall, recently modernized, is used for various functions; the Mobile County Library comes weekly, a bus twice weekly. There are two endowed charities—the Livingstone for £5, and the Hopkins for £10.

SULHAMSTEAD CHURCH

Sulhamstead is an oval-shaped scattered village, three miles across and more than twice as long, stretching from Burghfield Common northwards across the Bath Road, up to the wooded ridge of Englefield.

The present civil parish of Sulhamstead comprises the two ancient parishes of Sulhamstead Bannister Upper End and Sulhamstead Abbots.

The word Bannister preserves the family name of the knight, John Banastre, whose family first held the manor in about the year 1120. Bannister Church was under the jurisdiction of Pamber Priory, and when that was suppressed the priory and much of its property was given by the King to Queen's College, Oxford. From then until now the college has the right of appointment to the Rectory of Sulhampstead and some of the neighbouring parishes. Some of the flints from the recently demolished St. Michael's Church were used in the building of the new vestry at St. Mary Abbots.

Sulhamstead Abbots is so called because it was once under the jurisdiction of the Abbot of Reading Abbey. All that is left of the original Norman church is the font. The church was first dedicated to St. Bartholomew, then came the Black Death, and the villagers, perhaps in a "last ditch" desperate plea for mercy re-dedicated their church to the Mother of Our Lord and it became St. Mary's.

The only remaining inn, the Three and Jacks Booth, on the Bath Road, was once a busy coaching inn, and there are many differing stories concerning the name. The most likely links it with Jack of Newbury, the wealthy cloth merchant, who undoubtedly would have spent a lot of time travelling the Bath Road to and from London, but what or who were the "three"?

140

Sulhamstead House, a white Ionic porticoed house looking over the beautiful Kennet Valley was built in 1744 by David May and the estate comprised 1,800 acres. In 1952 it became the Berkshire Constabulary County Headquarters, and in 1968, following the amalgamation of five forces, it became the Thames Valley Police Training School. The garden boasts a 600-year-old Cedar of Lebanon.

The village is fortunate in having a number of beautiful and interesting houses and gardens, among them Folly Farm, a fine example of a Lutyens house; the Old Rectory—a William and Mary house—and Tyle Mill, all of which regularly open their gardens to the public.

The Kennet and Avon Canal, now cleared from Reading to Sulhamstead Lock, provides moorings for many pleasure craft, and westwards towards Ufton Nervet it becomes the fisherman's paradise, their green umbrellas dotted along the banks creating a peaceful scene.

Unfortunately much of the natural beauty of the area has been marred by the erection of pylons and the extraction of gravel, but it is hoped that nature will eventually do her valuable work and camouflage these scars.

Sunningdale

is a rather straggling area joining the old village clustered round the church and the newer part, built up around the station about a mile away.

The name is probably Saxon in origin, meaning "the home of Sunna's people" and most of the village originally formed part of Windsor Forest, which formerly stretched from Windsor to Basingstoke. The earliest evidence of occupation is the existence of several Bronze Age barrows. One of these was excavated in 1901 and contained fragments of twenty-three cinery urns, some of which are now in Reading Museum.

Throughout history the main highway to the south-west appears to have passed through Sunningdale. The Roman Road from London to Silchester, locally known as the "Devil's Highway", crossed the River Thames at Staines, ran through the site of Virginia Water, Fort Belvedere and Coworth, then skirted the field behind Church Road, along the edge of the football field, and thence to Bagshot.

In medieval times there was a small struggling community of nuns at Broomhall, who gave hospitality to travellers on the bridle path from London to Salisbury. It was an outpost of the rich Chertsey Abbey, founded sometime in the 12th century, and maintained until the dissolution in 1535. In 1199 King John gave the little Norman Church at Sunninghill to the nuns. In the churchyard at Sunninghill is a yew tree, thought to be over 1,000 years old, and the Norman arch at the entrance to the church was found in the kitchen block of a large house locally and restored to its original position in 1926. After the dissolution, the estates of the nunnery fell to the crown, and were granted by letters patent to St. John's College, Cambridge, who still own the freehold of much of the land today.

The old milestones along both the A30 and the A329 indicate that the modern highways follow roughly the lines of the old turnpike roads. In the 18th century these roads through wild and desolate Windsor Forest and Bagshot Heath made the area an ideal hunting ground for highwaymen. William Davies, Claude Duval, Captain Snow and Parson Darby are all known to have carried out their infamous deeds in this vicinity.

It seems that the village is still keeping the tradition of being near the main highway, as the M3 motorway now crosses Chobham Common just over the Surrey border.

Coworth was occupied as far back as Saxon times, but the present mansion, Coworth Park, was built about 1800. Coworth Park Farm is an excellent example of a Tudor farmhouse, the front being almost unchanged since it was first built.

Fort Belvedere was built as a folly in 1755 by the 2nd Duke of Cumberland, and enlarged and used as a hunting lodge by George IV. The ruins in the grounds, which can be seen from the shore of Virginia Water, are part of an ancient temple transported here from Leptis Magna near Tripoli. Queen Victoria was a frequent visitor and a royal salute was fired annually on her birthday from the guns mounted outside the house. Edward VIII, when Prince of Wales, made his home here and carried out extensive modernisation of the interior. It was here that the abdication order was signed, and afterwards the King left through Coworth Park grounds in order to avoid the press and publicity. Prince Victor of Hohenloe, a nephew of Queen Victoria, lived at St. Bruno in Charters Road, and is buried in the churchyard at Sunningdale.

There are several other large houses in the district, some still used as private residences, but many are now taken over for other purposes: Sunningdale Park is used as a Civil Service College,

Silwood Park as a field Station for Imperial College, Charters as a research establishment for Vickers Ltd., and Coworth Park as a school. Others such as Dale Lodge and Broomfield Park have been demolished, but their names are remembered in the modern estates built on the sites.

The area was popularised in the late 17th century by the discovery of Chalybeate springs, and the Wells Hotel at Sunninghill was built for people to "take the waters", and this became very fashionable. Many of the streams in the area run brownish in colour even today, and this is still due to the mineral deposits; not, as so many people assume, to the dumping of rusty bicycles!

The district is well known, of course, for its proximity to Ascot Race Course, which was founded by Queen Anne, and to the Sunningdale Golf Course, which is the venue for many international golf meetings.

There are many magnificent trees in the area, some of which are quite rare specimens; and in the early summer the many-coloured rhododendrons and azaleas in all the gardens are a breathtaking sight.

Outside St. Francis School in South Ascot is a statue presented by Mrs. Bob Hope, the wife of the famous comedian. Old names of interest are Starveall Farm, Kiln Lane and Tinders Lane.

Sunningwell & Bayworth

These two pleasing villages, which lie only 3½ miles from Oxford on the south-western slopes of Boars Hill, were in Saxon times the original site of the great Abbey of Abingdon.

There is a legend that the Stert stream appeared miraculously in answer to a dying man's prayer, but the stream caused so much difficulty that the Abbey was finally built at its mouth near Abingdon. The Stert stream to this day causes trouble with excessive flooding as it makes its way to join the River Thames.

At the Dissolution of the Abbey in 1538, the Prior became Rector of Sunningwell, where the church, with its heptagonal porch and mixed Gothic and Renaissance styles is unique in English architecture.

John Jewel, Bishop of Salisbury, was Rector of Sunningwell in 1551, and another was Samuel Fell, famous Dean of Christchurch, who lived in the village from 1625 to 1649; he is buried with his family in the chancel.

Inside the church, look for the two rows of huge poppy-head bench ends, like busby hats; the fine medieval wooden transept screen, and the Elizabethan pulpit.

143

Bayworth possessed a fine Manor House in Tudor times, owned by the Baskerville family, and described by the 17th-century historian, Anthony Wood, as "private and alone in a romancy place".

By 1722 the house was a ruin, but much of the material, including beams and woodwork, was used to build the present Manor farmhouse. Mr. R. G. Deane, who lives there, is one of a family that has farmed in the district for 500 years. There are many families in the village whose names go back 250 years . . . the Greens, Viners, Turners and Honeys are among them, and the verger of Sunningwell Church is 87-year-old Sarah Honey, whose work this has been for 54 years.

The Benedictine monks built the Manor of Sunningwell and used it as a hospice and resthouse, until the Dissolution. Elizabeth I frequently stayed there, and the old chapel is used as the dining-room today.

A recent owner, Mrs. Una Duval, has her own niche in modern history. A friend of Mrs. Pankhurst and her daughters, she was a member of the Woman's Suffrage Movement who chained herself to the railings of Buckingham Palace; she also served a prison sentence, went on hunger strike and was forcibly fed.

In 1972 a new school was opened in Sunningwell, and the old school is now used as a School of Arts and Crafts.

Sunningwell has a good Village Hall, recently extended and modernised with the support of the whole village; there is a post office store, and a public house called The Flowing Well which until 21 years ago was the rector's house.

Cricket has been played in the village for 100 years, the children still keep up the May Day revels, and the ancient crafts of chair caning and basketry are practised still in Sunningwell and Bayworth.

Sutton Courtenay

Here is a really beautiful village to visit. It lies on an arm of the Thames three miles south-east of Abingdon, the old centre of church, inns and interesting houses built round a green. There are noble trees, splendid gardens, and a general feeling of well-being. Some of the oldest houses—beamed, brick or mellow stone—which turn bland faces to the main road have gardens behind that run down to the river.

A footpath leads to the river and the weir with its small bridge, and here artists, photographers and bird-watchers all find a pleasant place to wander on a sunny day.

In Domesday, Sutton was a royal residence, and the Conqueror himself came here occasionally; his daughter-in-law, Queen Matilda, wife of Henry I, stayed here for the birth of her first child.

A complex of buildings made up the royal court, and one of these is now part of the Manor House, lying between the Green and the river. It is a timber-built house, of many periods, medieval, Tudor and Restoration, and some notably fine old yew trees grow in its extensive garden. There is also a splendid hornbeam avenue, planted by Mrs. Norah Lindsay, who lived at the Manor in the early part of this century.

The Courtenays, another family with royal connections, built the stone Norman Hall between 1190 and 1200; it has been altered from time to time, but is still a building of great interest.

Another 14th-century house, known as the Abbey, is approached from the Green through an avenue of great elms. Many prominent statesmen and ecclesiastics have used this house, as part of their salaries came from being Rectors of Sutton in the days of plural livings. The village would gain little from such priests, who only paid fleeting visits, using the Rectory House as a staging-post on their journeys.

One of these great prelates was Thomas Bekynton, Secretary to King Henry VI; his emblem, a fire-beacon and a barrel or tun (a play on his name) is carved over the church porch, and his name is remembered in Bekynton House, one of Sutton Courtenay's many very attractive houses.

The church near the Green reflects most phases of English architecture from the 12th to the 16th century, and is well worth a visit.

In the churchyard are the graves of the first Earl and Countess of Oxford and Asquith, who built the large house called The Wharf near the river, and lived in Sutton Courtenay both while he was Prime Minister and afterwards in retirement.

George Orwell, the writer, is also buried here, and there is a headstone to Mrs. Martha Pye, who died in 1822 aged 117 years. She is said to have walked to Abingdon when 100 years old!

Sutton Courtenay is a large village . . . from the central heart it spreads along a winding way of cottages, fine houses, and a few shops.

On the outskirts are large new housing estates, not much integrated with the old village; and a very fine village hall, much in demand for a great range of functions.

Towering over the boundary of the village is the great white giant sculpture of the new Didcot Power Station. It is the ultimate expression of the 20th century in a village that has weathered a thousand years.

Thatcham

Once a Royal Manor, and valued in Domesday book at £34 a year, Thatcham is now a busy community on the outskirts of Newbury.

In 1125 Thatcham Church was given to Reading Abbey, and later Henry II issued three charters compelling the men of the village to attend Thatcham Church or be fined; he also confirmed the weekly market held locally. A town fair was held from medieval times until 1888, and during the reign of Edward III the growing small town was classed as one of the four Boroughs of Berkshire, the others being Windsor, Wallingford and Reading.

The Black Death decimated the population of Thatcham, and it never recovered its importance in the county.

In modern times the village is growing again . . . with a population over 10,000, industry in the shape of the world-wide Reed Paper Group, and the proximity of the M4, Thatcham is no longer a rural community. There is still a local wood-turning industry, but the chief countryside attraction is the nearby Kennet and Avon Canal, which enthusiastic volunteers keep clear for recreational boating, angling, and nature observation.

Theale

Like many another Berkshire settlement Theale had Roman and Saxon predecessors, but the village of today is largely a modern development.

Until 1832 Theale was part of the large parish of Tilehurst, whose Rector was the famous Dr. Martin Routh, of Magdalene College, Oxford. It now has its own parish church, also a United Reformed church, and a new Roman Catholic church.

The great days of the village came with the stage coaches along the Bath Road, when every coachman had a favourite stopping place for refreshment and the changing of horses. This led to the building of seven or more inns around the area, and the unsavoury nickname of "Little Soddom" was given to the place.

The stage coaches went their way, and the motor cars arrived, the Bath Road became the A4, but Theale continued to be a favourite stopping place. There are fewer inns now, but quite sufficient for the constant flow of travellers.

In 1901 the population of Theale was under 1,000, and is more than doubled today. The war years brought great changes . . . the old craftsmen disappeared, including the saddler, the hurdle and besom maker, several carpenters, the village sweep and others. Factories have moved into Theale and the rural character has almost gone.

The M4 motorway has now brought more changes, but the people of Theale hope for more peace and less traffic on the old Bath Road, and something of a return to tranquillity.

Three Mile Cross

"A long, straggling, winding street, at the bottom of a fine eminence, with a road through it, always abounding in carts, horsemen, and carriages, and lately enlivened by a stage-coach . . ." so wrote Mary Russel Mitford of Three Mile Cross, to which she had moved with her parents on 5th April, 1820.

The road through the village is still a busy one, and with the M4 motorway skirting the village, so it will continue.

"The elegant town of B——," wrote Miss Mitford, describing the view from part of the village, "with its fine old church towers and spires; the whole view shut in by a range of chalky hills; and over every part of the picture, trees so profusely scattered that it appears like a woodland scene, with glades and villages intermixed . . ." Poor Miss Mitford, lover of peace and unchanging country ways, what would she say of that view today?

The move to Three Mile Cross was a sad occasion for Mary, then aged 32, for the family had been forced, through financial crises caused through her father's passion for gambling, to leave Bertram House at Grazely, where she wrote in her diary that evening, "and went to live in Mr. Body's cottage at The Cross. Very sorry to go. In a great skirmish all day long. Very uncomfortable indeed." This remained their modest home, and Mary stayed on another nine years until she moved, for the last few years of her life, to be near her long-standing friend Lady Russel at nearby Swallowfield.

If it had not been for Dr. Mitford's extravagance and the resultant persistent financial chaos, Three Mile Cross might never have become one of the most famous villages to appear in print.

Although she had always kept a diary, it was not until the responsibility of supporting her parents fell on her shoulders that Mary began to produce the gay and charming work for which she gained fame, and which, 150 years later, gives us perhaps the truest, certainly one of the most delightful, pictures of ordinary country life in early and mid-19th century England. The sketches she wrote originally appeared in the *Lady Magazine*—the best of them being later gathered into the volume, *Our Village*. Although based on Three Mile Cross, which in time she came to love, and which certainly loved her, the sketches portray country life as a whole.

Her cottage still stands, though, sadly, in a very dilapidated state. "Did I tell you," she wrote to Elizabeth Barrett on December 15th, 1837, "I shall have a pretty upstairs sitting room, 13 ft. square, with a little ante-room lined with books, both looking on to the garden?" For, at that time, alterations were being made to the cramped four-roomed house, and thus it is today essentially what it was during the last 15 years of her occupation.

Not so, alas, her beloved garden, where she entertained so many friends known in literary and theatrical circles, and which she tended so lovingly; ". . . full of common flowers, tulips, pinks, larkspur . . . with an arbour of privet, not unlike a sentry box, where one lives in a delicious green light, and look out on the gayest of all gay flower-beds . . ."; all that is gone, replaced by a mission hall!

The Swan Inn still serves the needs of the thirsty locals, but the ". . . carts, waggons and return chaises" are replaced in the forecourt by bikes, Minis and Mercedes, whose drivers are perhaps refreshing themselves (within limits!) before joining the nearby M4.

Here is the same wheelwright's cottage, but it is no longer "the curate's lodgings . . .". A little way up the hill is the house described as "the red cottage of the lieutenant, covered with vines, the very image of comfort and content", but it is now whitewashed and the lieutenant no longer leans on the gate. At the top of the hill is Hill House, but where is ". . . the old thorn, such a thorn, so elegant, so lightsome and yet so rich?"

In Miss Mitford's day Three Mile Cross, separated from Reading and neighbouring villages by open country, was almost entirely self-sufficient; there was the shoemaker, "pale, sickly looking", the blacksmith doubling as constable, the carpenter "famed ten miles round", as well as the wheelwright, and of course the village shop, ". . . repository for bread, shoes, tea, cheese, tape, ribbons and bacon; for everything, in short, except the one particular thing which you happen to want at the moment. . . ."

When she set out on one of her many expeditions she would have passed the stocks, on the little green near the duckpond at the corner of Church Lane. An all too frequent sight would have been the procession of prisoners being taken to Reading Assizes or (a spectacle that cast a gloom on the usually cheerful village population) unfortunates taking their last terrifying walk towards the gallows in town.

Woodcock Lane was once a favourite haunt of courting couples, and here also the gypsies made their regular seasonal halt. Miss Mitford has left us a picture of her first sight of them. ". . . they had pitched their tent under one of the oak-trees . . . an old crone, in a tattered red cloak and black bonnet, who was stooping over a kettle, a pretty, black-eyed girl, at work under the trees; a sunburnt urchin collecting sticks and dead leaves to feed their out-of-door fire. . . ." It takes a person of determination to negotiate the lane now; overgrown and deeply rutted, it is scheduled as part of a relief road for the village.

At the end of Church Lane stands St. Mary's Church, Shinfield, and one can imagine Miss Mitford's frequent visits to this ancient church, last resting-place of her parents, to whom she had dedicated so much of her health and working life. Did she decide to write *Belford Regis* as she travelled, by pony chaise, into Reading one summer afternoon?

One thing is certain. If Mary Mitford went shopping in "Belford Regis" today she would return to her cottage in Three Mile Cross a bewildered little lady. But, despite the roundabouts and "multistoreys", the bingo halls and supermarkets, she would still find enough material to fill a hundred notebooks.

Tutts Clump is a tiny hamlet between Bradfield and Bucklebury, hardly more than a scattering of pretty cottages.

The delightful place name is thought to come from a tree surmounted mound opposite the Traveller's Rest, where a General Tutts rested his horses before the Battle of Newbury during the Civil Wars.

At the same mound St. Birinus is said to have rested on a pilgrimage, and when he stuck his sword into the ground it became alight.

In a steep lane called Rotten Row are several beautiful old black and white cottages; an old village inn called The Slipper is now a private house known as Farthings. It was named by the Temple Thurston family, who were told to "save their farthings" and they could have a country cottage.

Brick houses in the district have been built of locally made bricks, although the kilns are now disused.

Bradfield Hall, a late 18th-century brick house with a clock tower and a good painted ceiling by Adam is mentioned in the section headed Bradfield.

Tutts Clump has a small Methodist Chapel with the foundation stone dated 1879.

Twyford

A glance at the map will show the visitor how Twyford, two fords, came to be named. The Loddon and other tributaries join and break away in a network of small waterways, and the point at which these could be crossed most easily would encourage settlers. When the pack horse was superseded by the four-wheeled coach this junction was still important for the traveller. Turnpike milestones and pumps for watering the horses as well as laying the dust can still be noticed by the observant, erected by the roadside.

Twyford is on the main London to Bath highway. The by-pass was opened very nearly a century after the railway which arrived in 1838.

The pleasant group of almshouses were built in 1640 by Sir Richard Harrison, lord of the manor of Whistley. Over the porch is carved the motto, "Deo et pauperinud", "For God and the poor", a reminder that few of the residents would trouble to translate today. The room on the right of the lobby used to be the Court House of the manor when it sat to administer local justice. The old oak screen between the Court Room and the lobby is worth looking at.

Polehampton Schools. There is a story that on Christmas Eve about the year 1666 a destitute boy named Edward Polehampton was befriended by the landlord of the former Rose and Crown Inn, who gave him food, clothing and shelter and helped him on his way to London. Polehampton prospered and grew rich. On his death he bequeathed a charity to benefit the poor boys of the village. Wee Waif Inn on the Bath Road was named after Edward Polehampton.

Dr. William Gordon-Stables of "The Jungle", Ruscombe Road, Twyford, was known as the first gentleman gipsy. He was born in 1840 and became the Founder President of the Caravan Club in 1907. His fame rested on the huge horse-drawn saloon caravan christened "The Wanderer" that he took on 700-mile cruises to the West of England and to Scotland. This interesting antique has found a resting-place in Bristol Museum.

A towering landmark, as you enter the village from the Old Bath Road, stands Twyford Mill. Although the present structure is not particularly ancient, there has been a mill on this spot from early times. In 1810 two brothers from Macclesfield, Cheshire, built a silk mill here, to be followed by a flour mill, and nowadays by a factory to process cattle cake.

The outstanding beauty of Twyford, which the rushing motorist can enjoy as well as the leisurely pedestrian, is Waterer's Floral Mile. It borders each side of the A4. There are several other firms who have discovered the richness of the Thames Valley soil, and beds of lovely coloured flowers grown for their seeds, as well as a multitude of entrancing roses and plants to whet the appetite of the gardener fill the fields that edge the motorway.

Uffington This pleasant old settlement in the Vale of the White Horse may not be the most beautiful of the many downland villages, but more than any other it is secure in its place in literature.

It is the village from which Tom Brown set off for his schooldays at Rugby, and where his creator, Thomas Hughes, was born.

Uffington Brook encircles the village, and until quite recent years was the only source of water. The fine Carolean Schoolhouse still stands almost in the churchyard, just as it did in Tom Brown's day; and the beautiful 13th-century church of St. Mary should not be missed. It is unusually large and impressive for so small a village, and is locally known as the Cathedral of the Vale.

A mile to the north of Uffington the residents of Baulking still exercise their age-old right to graze their livestock on the village green. There are several delightful Queen Anne houses, and in a meadow behind one of them the great hunter-steeplechaser Baulking Green enjoyed honourable retirement until his death in 1978. The tiny church of St. Nicholas is well worth a visit. Vale villages tend to be rather stark, but tiny Woolstone, to the south of Baulking, is wrapped in a positive bower of trees, and is a treasure house to the botanist and ornithologist. This is a small gem, a picture-book place of neat cottages and gay gardens, a clear running stream and and a small old church on a hill-top.

For the tired traveller there is a fine Elizabethan inn, aptly called the White Horse.

The three villages of Uffington, Baulking and Woolstone lie just off A417 between Wantage and Faringdon.

Ufton Nervet

The parish of Ufton Nervet occupies a strip of land four miles long and about one and a half miles wide in its broadest part, between Sulhamstead and Padworth, stretching from the Burghfield–Kingsclere road to beyond the Bath Road.

Ufton (or Offetone) is mentioned in Domesday Book. The church itself is modern, having been rebuilt by Mr. Richard Benyon in 1861, but it contains many ancient monuments including memorials to the Perkins family of the 16th and 17th centuries. The ivy-covered ruin of the little chapel of Ufton Richard may be seen close to the old pound, and almost opposite the Dog and Partridge which was converted into a private residence several years ago.

Grimm's Bank—and the ditch—show themselves on the southern boundary of the parish.

At the end of its lovely broad avenue of oaks stands Ufton Court, with a great old barn, outbuildings and cottages; and on the south side its terrace, old walled garden and fishponds. Although it dates from the 15th century, the present Elizabethan house was built in the shape of a letter "E" with a few later additions. From the 15th century until 1782 the property was owned by the Perkyns (later Perkins) family. They were Roman Catholic recusants, and in the days of Queen Elizabeth I many priests found sanctuary there. The entrances to the famous priests' hiding holes are still intact, though the exits have been blocked up. In 1838 the Ufton Estate was sold to Mr. Benyon de Beauvon. The widow of Richard Perkyns remarried Sir John Marvyn of Fountell Giffard in Wiltshire, but maintained her connection with Ufton. She died in 1581 and in her will provided for a yearly distribution to the "poore" of Ufton of ". . . Good and Howshoulde Bread", "canvas of twelve pence the all" and "blewe clothe of twenty pence the yards". This bequest has been faithfully administered. Bread and (except during the last war) house linen has been given to the parishioners of Ufton by the trustees of the Marvyn Charity, through the same window in the hall of Ufton Court at mid-Lent, for the past 398 years.

The village school, built in 1870 and modernized in the early 1960's, is now known as the Sulhamstead and Ufton Parochial School.

The country through which the River Kennet flows is still very peaceful; pheasants and partridges—dispersed with a flurry by the occasional skulking fox—forage for food, as they have always done, in Cow Pond Piece, Nan Pie and the Rod Beds.

Wallingford

Perhaps this proud and ancient Borough does not strictly belong in a Village Book, but it is the centre of all the Thames Valley settlements in this part of the county, and the history of Berkshire is written into its very stones.

Its position on the Icknield Way and at a natural ford on the River Thames made it the chief town on the direct east to west route for travellers from the Bronze Age to the 20th Century.

Kings and Queens through the ages have known Wallingford and stayed in its castle . . . Danish Sweyn burnt it, Edward the Confessor rebuilt it, William the Conqueror marched his army over its ford, Queen Matilda fled over the frozen river to sanctuary here, Henry II granted its Great Charter, Henry VIII and his whole court spent summers here, Queen Elizabeth rebuilt the old bridge with stones from the Priory that her father had destroyed. Walk about the old streets and through Market Place and there are interesting features on every side. The lovely little Town Hall was built in 1670, with a pillared first storey that once held stocks and whipping posts, and a great chamber above, painted and gilded and the pride of the town. Among the dignatories portrayed in the Town Hall is Sir William Blackstone, 1723–1780, great man of law, who lived in Wallingford and is buried in St. Peter's Church.

A terrible fire destroyed much of the medieval architecture, so Wallingford has mainly 17th and 18th-century buildings. The old George Inn belongs to an earlier age, and is a fine example of a coaching inn built round a courtyard. The great castle was destroyed in the Civil Wars, but fragments of its massive stone walls remain.

The natural glory of Wallingford is the river, a waterway for every sort of craft, and a playground for the townsfolk and visitors.

Wallingford once had 15 churches, of which only three remain, but the names are kept alive in the little winding streets . . . St. Rumbold, St. Martin, St. John and St. Nicholas.

Drive over the beautiful Wallingford bridge from the east and you will find endless things of interest to investigate and enjoy

STOCKS AT WHITE WALTHAM.

Waltham St. Lawrence

Most of the villages in Berkshire claim Saxon ancestry, with some Roman connections, but Waltham St. Lawrence boasts an unusual hexagonal Romano-English Temple, clearly seen in an aerial photograph. It is not surprising to find that Roman and pre-Roman remains are still being found in abundance. The invading Saxons destroyed the original settlement in the 7th century. Waltham comes from the Saxon meaning "Unsteady House or Home".

The church, mentioned in the Domesday Book, was part of Geoffrey de Mandeville's reward for supporting the Conqueror. The Advowson, regarded as a source of income, was passed over to the Prior of Hurley when the Norman Baron decided to found a monastery, as an act of piety. The fabric of the church shows by its various styles the many alterations it has undergone. There are 11th-century rounded arches, 14th-century side-aisles and chancel, and 16th-century east window and upper stages of the tower. The base of the tower has a special cupboard for the regalia and banners used in medieval processions. There is also a fragment of early wall painting which has escaped the whitewashing of Puritan enthusiasts.

Among notable people who lived in Waltham are the Newbury family. They commuted to run a printing business in London for

400 years. The Newburys left to the village the magnificent 15th-century Bell Inn, which stands near the church adjoining the village pound. They had bought the lordship of the manor from the See of Winchester and eventually sold it to the Neville family in 1608. The Newbury's original home was at Beenhams, now demolished, but it is clear that it was once a moated manor house.

The Civil War, followed by the Commonwealth, split the village deeply. The Neville brothers fought on opposite sides. The Vicar remained royalist, although the principal families were predominantly Parliamentarians. It is reputed that when Beenhams was demolished in the 19th century a skeleton of a royalist soldier in full soldier's accoutrement was discovered. The parish register records the burials of a number of soldiers from both sides. At one time Sir Thomas Foot, a 17th-century Lord Mayor of London, rented the house. He is remembered in the village, partly for a charity he set up and partly for the correspondence he had with the Vicar over a feud.

Two of the finest houses surviving today are Paradise and Borlases (originally known as Blazes). Not only do the two houses back on each other, but members of the families who lived in them, Sharpes and Deanes, married each other in two successive generations.

More recently, the village was the home of William and Ernest Renshaw. Few people realise that these twin brothers were regarded by their contemporaries as the creators of modern lawn tennis. For ten years, from 1880, they dominated the tennis world by winning every major singles and doubles event open to them. Before their arrival on the scene, lawn tennis was regarded as an inferior field of exercise for those who did not have opportunity to gain skill at racquets.

Today, Waltham St. Lawrence, which incorporates Shurlock Row, is a thriving and active community, with a wealth of picturesque houses and historical associations to delight the traditionalist and modernist alike.

Wantage

This beautiful old Berkshire town is a centre for numerous small downland villages, and one of the most ancient settlements in the country.

King Alfred the Great was born and educated here in 849, and his heroic statue stands in the Market Place, a slightly smaller version of the one at Winchester which became his capital.

According to the plaque on his monument, Alfred advanced learning, modified the law, remodelled the army, and founded the navy. He also was the first British leader to rout the Danes, although a later generation of invaders burnt his birthplace to the ground in 1006.

Wantage today is a clean, open small town, built round a Market Square, with some fine Georgian red brick buildings and neat Victorian terraces. On market days the square is crowded with stalls and shoppers, and at other times the pleasant open space is packed with cars.

It is fitting that Alfred's town should still be a place of learning, and Wantage is known for its many fine schools, both old and new, state schools, private schools and convents.

The Wantage Sisters of the Community of St. Mary the Virgin were founded in 1847 in a small cottage in Newbury Street; today the mother house is the Belmont Convent, St. Katherine's Home is for the elderly, and a large boarding school for girls, St. Mary's, is built on high ground to the west of Wantage.

The parish church of St. Peter and St. Paul is one of the most beautiful in Berkshire. It sits just off the Market Place in a quiet close, and should not be missed by the visitors to the town.

Much of the fabric is 13th-century, and the 15th-century chantry, which was given to the church by the Trade Guilds of Wantage, is now a Lady Chapel. The Lord of the Manor in 1450 was Lord Fitzwarren, whose daughter Alice married the same Dick Whittington, Lord Mayor of London, known to generations of pantomime lovers.

Warfield

A glance at the map will show that the ancient parish of Warfield lies anxiously in the Green Belt, to the north of Bracknell New Town. Already the southern quarter has been devoured by the developer, as Bracknell High Street was once part of Warfield parish. For centuries there were a straggle of houses, inhabited by the traders who settled along the street. They owed allegiance to the lord of the Manor of Warfield and attended St. Michael's Church, which was then in the middle of the manor, although 2½ miles away.

Visitors should not miss seeing the church of St. Michael's, one of the largest and best-preserved parish churches in Berkshire. Built on Saxon foundations, the four enlargements (built roughly about a century apart) are clearly distinguished by the four roofs. These additions blend smoothly with the medieval church, now the north aisle. The white chalk-stone chancel is most noteworthy. It was built by the Priors of Hurley (Patrons for 400 years) for use as their winter retreat, just before the Black Death of 1339 wiped out most of the population of the village. There are many unusual features such as an Angelus Tower, the remains of an Easter Sepulchre, and 15th-century stained glass set in the fine curvilinear stone tracery of the east window. There is also a Rood Loft, a peal of ten bells, and a magnificent modern organ. The Parish Room in the churchyard may date from the time when the monks came to Warfield and would require a cloister and workshops for their daily duties. The three Stew Ponds at the bottom of Rectory House were obviously designed to provide the Friday platters of fish.

There are several houses of architectural interest, and the parish is rich in timber-framed Elizabethan examples. St. Michael's Grange is one of the most interesting with its axial-chimney block rising through the centre of the house and the Regency additions. At one time it was owned by the clock-making family Horsnayle, and was later the residence of the Baron of Warfield, General Sir Edward Spears, friend of Sir Winston Churchill, and sponsor for General de Gaulle when France was on her knees before Hitler. His wife, whose nom-de-plume was Mary Borden, is buried in Warfield's churchyard. She was the authoress of many popular novels and war stories, and was the instigator of mobile hospitals in World War I. Both husband and wife wrote books of great interest on World War II.

Two turnpike roads pass through the parish from Reading to London, marked by the compulsory milestones. The one which meanders north and is part of the Forest Road from Winnersh to Cranbourne was used by the drovers who took their meat to Smithfield Market "on the hoof", before the advent of the railway.

There is a wonderful view from the top of Cabbage Hill across the Thames, and at its foot lies the beautifully proportioned Regency-style country house called Warfield Hall, standing in an extensive park. It was once the home of Sir Charles Brownlow, famous for his war record in China. On his retirement he was appointed A.D.C. to Queen Victoria and took to himself a wife from Warfield. He did much for the village, restoring the church tower and building what would be described today as a "Community Centre".

Some two miles from the church is Warfield Park. In the 18th century it was bought by Nabob, Colonel John Walsh, secretary and friend of Lord Clive and a member of the Royal Society. Here he built a large house, surrounded by well-laid-out gardens, grottoes and a park stocked by trees of foreign interest. The family rose in importance as they were drawn into court circles, finally acquiring the title of Lord Ormathwaite. There is a story that seven crowned heads sat down to dine at one of Lady Ormathwaite's extravagant Edwardian dinner parties. When the family could no longer afford to live at Warfield Park the estate was sold. As it was the beginning of World War II, the U.S.A. army took over the place and completed its downfall. It is now a flourishing caravan site.

Wargrave

Madame Tussaud lies buried in Wargrave churchyard. No, not *the* Madame of Waxworks fame, but her daughter-in-law. However, it seems appropriate that a person so closely connected with the originator of all those motionless monarchs should lie here in Wargrave, known to so many royal persons.

William's 1086 survey reports: "Weregrave . . . Edid held it . . ." Edid being Edith Edward the Confessor's Queen. Edward's mother, Queen Emma, was supposed to have lived in the village, the remains of her palace, in Church Street, being finally demolished in 1827. Queen Emma, because of suspicions aroused by the Archbishop, was accused by her son of too great intimacy with the Bishop of Winchester. Emma indignantly demanded the Ordeal by Fire, to prove her innocence, and this took place in Winchester Cathedral, where she spent the night before praying to St. Swithin.

The king watched his mother walk unscathed over nine red-hot plough shares, he himself receiving afterwards, as penance, stripes from the Bishop. The gossiping Archbishop was banished, the Queen Mother's confiscated property returned, and in gratitude, Emma presented to the Bishop one manor for every plough share she had walked over. So Wargrave came under the Lordship of the Bishops of Winton.

A later Queen, Elizabeth I, did not feel so amicably towards Winchester's Bishop. Annoyed by a sermon he preached before her, she relieved him of Wargrave, giving it instead to "our trusted Henry Nevill", with whose family it remained until the last century.

The A'Bear family is one of the earliest recorded in old deeds, and many properties such as Bear Place, Bear Ash, and Bear Hill bear witness to their influence.

The present white, bow-fronted, early 19th-century Manor looks across the river from its fine position and must have been a welcome retreat for George III and his family in 1804. Much of Park Place lies in Wargrave, and General Conway, one-time owner, built the rustic bridge on the Henley road with stones from Reading

Abbey. His daughter Anne was responsible for the two heads, representing Thamesis and Isis, on Henley bridge.

The village seems to have got off lightly in the Plague scourge in 1665, having only 14 victims; perhaps it was in gratitude that the villagers donated £2 1s. 11d. towards the suffering poor in the Great Fire a year later.

In the 18th century the extravagant Irish peer, the Earl of Barrymore, came to live just off the High Street, in a house now known as "Barrymore". In 1782 he built an elaborately fitted theatre close to his house, and installed Delphini of Covent Garden as permanent clown. The theatre cost over £60,000 and the first performance in 1791 was a gala night. London actors took the principal roles, and people of all ranks, including George IV, flocked from far and wide, especially in the summer months when a visit to this rural riverside village was well worth the often uncomfortable journey.

The rakish earl was not to enjoy his venture for long; he died suddenly in 1793 as the result of an accident while escorting French prisoners to Dover, and was buried in Wargrave Church chancel on a Sunday, so that his creditors could not seize his body and hold it for his debts. He had squandered £300,000 on theatrical and sporting activities, and his home was sold up and the theatre was pulled down.

A frequent performer at the theatre was Sir Morris Ximenes, who bought Bear Place. Sir Morris commanded the Wargrave Rangers in the Peninsular War, and he bought a row of cottages (now called the Barracks) for the 12 survivors of the troop.

A large mill used to stand near Hennerton backwater, and in dry summers traces of walls in the fields, and old piles in the water, are sometimes visible.

Lavender Cottage, still standing above the Henley road, was for over 100 years home to Zachary Allnutt, the lavender grower, and his family. The 40 acres of lavender, on both sides of the road, must have sweetened the air for some distance around, before it ended up in the not so fragrant streets of London. You can still enter the cool, dark cellars under the cottage, but the stills and apparatus for making the essence and lavender water, no longer stand there.

The Bull Inn and White Hart were both popular halts for the coaches that had turned off the busy Bath Road; the newer St. George and Dragon is probably better known, looking on to the Thames, and with its celebrated sign. Now kept inside the inn, it was painted by Royal Academicians G. D. Leslie and J. Hodgson, with St. George on one side fighting the Dragon, and on the other downing a welcome tankard of beer after his efforts!

About 700 people lived in the village in mid-16th century; now, after extensive building developments, the population tops 4,000.

In 1861 Robert Piggott died leaving a Trust for ". . . 24 girls and 24 boys to be educated in reading, writing and religious knowledge". The school still stands, with additions and alterations, above the village. The children used to wear "Piggott clothes"— navy serge dresses with red cloaks for girls; knee breeches, yellow waistcoats and Norfolk jackets for boys—and very colourful they must have looked.

The Piggott Trust is no more, but Founders Day is observed annually at the Secondary Modern School on the Twyford road, where 600 seniors from Wargrave and surrounding villages attend. The infants and junior schools in the village take another 300 from Wargrave only.

The Rev. Henry Sellon left a sum, in 1793, to provide £10 annually to "a serving man and a maid servant", alternatively, natives of Wargrave, who had stayed three years in one "place".

Wargrave's greatest benefactor was Mrs. Henrietta Smith, who lived in a house called Woodclyffe, which she left to be a convalescent home. She donated the Woodclyffe Hall in the High Street, where most public functions take place, in memory of her husband, being opened with ceremony in 1900. £1,500 was endowed for its upkeep, and a village clock was added to the front in 1970, from an endowment by the late Irvine Rankin. This generous lady also provided almshouses, allotments, a hostel (on the site of Queen Emma's palace), recreation ground, and electric light in the church and Mission Hall.

Boat businesses flourish on the river-bank, often connected with one family for many years. A ferry enables Wargrave and Shiplake to combine, once a year, to hold the now famous regatta. *Three Men in a Boat* and George Formby's *Keep Fit* were partly filmed in a Wargrave backwater.

And so back to the churchyard, and St. Mary's Church, founded in A.D. 900, on Mill Green where, Domesday reported, were 12 elms worth 4d. each.

Whitsunday, 1914, was a black day in the story of Wargrave. On that day, one of the foremost Feast Days of the church, a militant group of Suffragettes set fire to St. Mary's and partly destroyed the ancient building, apart from the Norman tower heightened with Tudor bricks. Some ancient chalk arches were saved, and later rebuilt in the north wall, but the fine Jacobean pulpit and all the memorials were reduced to ashes. The church plate was snatched from the flames, as were the old registers dating from 1537, and including such fascinating village names as Pocket, Knife, Rolls, Butter, and Sally Lunn.

The new church, built as closely as possible to the old plans, was reopened in 1916, and one wonders whether the congregation could have imagined, on that wartime Sunday, when women were still without the vote, the sort of life their grand-daughters would be living in Wargrave and elsewhere half a century on.

But then, remember brave Queen Emma! Perhaps Wargrave has always been used to women of independence!

Wash Common

on the west of Newbury is really part of the old market town, but lies on higher ground, on the open heath land between the Kennet and Enborne valleys, and has some of the feeling of a separate village.

It was on this sparsely populated tableland that the first battle of Newbury was fought in 1643, and many of the older streets of Wash Common have names that link them with this turbulent past. Essex Street, Charles Street, Stuart Road, Battery End, Cary Close and Falkland Road are all reminders of those unhappy days.

The Falkland Memorial at the junction of Essex Street and Andover Road commemorates that Lord Falkland who lost his life in the battle. His body was carried to Falkland Farm, and local legend says that his ghost still haunts the place. It was here also that Sir Jacob Astley, fighting on the King's side, prayed his famous little prayer: "O Lord, I may be very busy today, I may forget Thee, but please do Thou not forget me".

The great oaks that once grew on Wash Common were widely used for building, and it is claimed that 16th-century ships which fought the Spanish Armada contained Berkshire oak from these heathlands. It is sure that the original wooden bridge in Northbrook Street, Newbury, was sturdily constructed from local trees.

Today the whole district is purely residential, with a number of schools, churches, social clubs and a lively community spirit.

WELFORD PARK.

Welford

The Lambourn Valley has no more attractive village than Welford, built round the splendid Queen Anne mansion, Welford Park. The parish, which spreads over 5,000 acres with the small population of 750 people, includes the village of Wickham and the hamlets Hoe Benham, Easton and Weston.

The Roman Ermin Street passes through the parish, and coins and pottery have been found locally. In A.D. 686 the Saxon King of Wessex, Caedwalla, granted Welford and Wickham to the Monastery of Abingdon.

The M4 motorway now divides Welford from Wickham, and the old bridges over the Lambourn River are now dwarfed by the massive flyover carrying the great road.

Welford Park, set in beautifully wooded parklands, with deer park, swift-flowing river and drifts of snow-drops, bluebells and daffodils in their seasons, was built in 1702 by the famous architect, Thomas Archer.

An earlier house had been a hunting lodge of Henry VIII until 1546, when it was granted to Sir Thomas Parry, faithful Treasurer of the household of Princess Elizabeth during her stormy girlhood. This house was later sold to Sir Francis Jones, a Lord Mayor of London.

The Archer family lived in their grand new house until 1770, when the heiress Susannah Archer married Jacob Houblon, and their son took the name of Archer-Houblon. This family remained at Welford Park until 1954, when the present owner inherited it from her uncle.

The lovely little church of St. Gregory stands near the great house, and was very much rebuilt by the Rev. W. Nicholson in 1852–55. Much of the fabric was retained in the new building, including the rare round tower with octagonal spire . . . the Victorian restorers carefully marked every stone and faithfully placed it in its right place in the new church.

Wickham In the sister village of Wickham is a particularly interesting church dedicated to St. Swithun, with a Saxon tower of great antiquity and tremendously thick walls of flint and mortar. The tower had been used as a beacon and was once separated from the church, but that zealous restorer, the Rev. W. Nicholson, rebuilt the nave and sanctuary and incorporated the old tower in the new church.

Perhaps the busy gentleman's most original contribution to St. Swithun's is the famous Elephant Chapel. The interior roof is of carved oak, there are eight angels in the nave carved in lime wood, and eight splendid papier mâché elephants in the north aisle. Mr. Nicholson brought three elephants from the Paris Exhibition of 1862 and set them up as examples of Fortitude, Docility and Strength for all to admire. He regarded them as just as appropriate as angels in his church. Later, five copies were made in this country, bringing the full troupe up to eight.

Two pew ends in the centre aisle were designed by Sir George Gilbert Scott, and the font cover was brought from New Zealand. The font near the door is very ancient, and was dug up near the church early this century.

Welford and Wickham, remote, peaceful and very picturesque, are well worth visiting on a sunny day of exploration in the Lambourn Valley.

The Village, Windsor Great Park This attractive modern

village is sited in the heart of Windsor Great Park.

Until 1948 the small community living in the Park was widely scattered, forestry workers, gamekeepers and gatekeepers living in splendid isolation.

A few houses clustered round Prince Consort's workshops which had been designed by the Prince Consort about 1850, and consisted of stabling for cart horses, a saw mill driven by water power, and carpenters' and joiners' shops.

During and after the second world war, activities in the Park had considerably increased—1,500 acres of land was now being farmed, there was a large gardening area of 600 acres including the Savill and new Valley gardens, and an ever-growing acreage of woodlands. This meant that there had to be a great increase in the number of employees on the estate. These men had to travel several miles to work, either on foot or bicycle from outlying villages.

King George VI, who was on the throne at the time, had always taken a great interest in the development of the Park and the welfare of the employees, and it was at his instigation that the first thoughts of a real village in the Park arose.

The King's wishes were readily accepted by the Commissioners of Crown Lands who are responsible for the management of the Windsor Estate.

Architects were engaged to design the new village, which was to be sited near the main centre of activity—Prince Consort's workshops, where many of the men worked. They were instructed to vary design, materials, roof lines and aspect. These conditions were most successfully achieved, resulting in in a country village full of character.

To complete the village, a charmingly designed shop-cum post office was built as well as a fine community centre surrounded by spacious playing fields. This centre was called the York Hall to commemorate the great interest which the Duke and Duchess of York (later King George VI and Queen Elizabeth) had taken in the daily life of the Park.

The village, consisting of 24 houses, was completed in 1948, and there was no difficulty in finding tenants for the attractive modern homes.

A few years later, with a new increase of employees, a further 24 houses were added to the original village.

Although the village is of no historical interest, the care and thought put into its design and building, and the skilful way it has been planned to blend in with the old trees and open spaces which surround it, have made it an outstanding example of modern development.

Old Windsor

The name of Old Windsor conjures up a town of great antiquity, but the truth is that though it was a Saxon town, the largest in Berkshire, the Normans undermined its importance by building their great fortress on the outcrop of rock above the river, some two miles to the north-west.

The Saxons found the Thames a convenient highway, and a settlement developed as the richness of the alluvial plain was exploited, and a township grew up. A few miles to the south-east is another alluvial plain known to every school child as the place where the Magna Charter was signed, famous Runnymede. Close by is the simple Portland stone plinth raised in memory of the murdered President of America, John Kennedy.

At Cooper's Hill, high on the crest of the scarp slope which runs from Staines to end abruptly with the enchanted castle of Windsor, stands the Commonwealth Air Forces Memorial. This is dedicated to the memory of the airmen who have no marked grave, and is beautifully sited with a magnificent view across the basin of the Thames. It was opened by Queen Elizabeth II in 1952.

The parish church of St. Peter and St. Andrew follows the usual Berkshire pattern. The original Saxon church was destroyed, to be rebuilt in 1216 and restored in 1863 by Sir George Gilbert Scott. There are many fine brasses to the Michell family, a reminder of the close association of the people of Old Windsor with the Castle.

Most of Windsor Great Park lies within the parish, including the remarkable 2½-mile avenue from the castle to the statue of George III, clothed in a Roman toga, astride the enormous Copper Horse. This "Long Walk" was planned by Charles II and cost him £5,000, and that was 300 years ago! With special places for the picnickers, the greater part of the Park is now open to the public, a privilege granted only a little more than a century ago. Before 1930 there were no gardens at all in the Great Park, but today the Savill Garden and the Punchbowl, in the Valley Garden, where the azaleas spiral the slopes, are a truly wonderful sight. The last weeks of April and early May when the shrubs burst into colour is the most rewarding time for a visit. The landscaping of the 200 acres from Smith's Lawn to Virginia Water was a dream that came true almost by chance. Labour-saving varieties of growing things were offered to the Park, when Wexham Place was sold, such as the plants for the Heather Garden round Smith's Lawn. It is on the Lawn, not far from the Copper Horse, that polo matches are played most weekends, often attended by royalty in a relaxed mood.

Of the many famous houses in the parish, probably the best known is Beaumont College, once a Roman Catholic Public School for Boys. It is now a Training School for International Computers. It has associations with Henry Thynne and Warren Hastings, and Queen Victoria visited the school three times. The old Union Workhouse, sad monument to misapplied philanthropy, has been taken over by the Windsor Hospital Management Committee and is now a Geriatric Unit and an Old People's Home.

Winkfield

is said to be the second largest parish in England and takes a great arable area of Windsor Forest, with several widely separated hamlets . . . North Street, The Plain, Maidens Green, Brock Hill, Winkfield Row and Chavey Down.

With vigilance and a strict enforcement of the Green Belt policy, the village is fighting to keep this corner of Berkshire rural, instead of becoming a soulless dormitory merging with Bracknell New Town and North Ascot.

There are some fine old buildings and interesting houses to see . . . St. Mary's Church, dating from the 13th and 14th centuries, the old Court House, now the White Hart Inn; the Old Rectory, the Abbey Farm and Abbey Gate house; Knights Hall in Winkfield Lane, the old Forge and the Pump Room; Handpost Farm and Keepers Cottage and Tile Cottage at Winkfield Row.

Here is a favourite place for fashionable schools, and Winkfield Place is now the setting for expensive young girls learning the Constance Spry ways with flowers, cookery and the more esoteric domestic arts. Lambrook School in Winkfield Row is a Boys' Preparatory School, and Heathfield School on the London Road a boarding school for girls.

Once farmers or foresters, the people of Winkfield now tend to work in the neighbouring towns or commute to London. There is one interesting new Space Age Industry . . . the Tracking Station on Pigeon House Lane receives and records information from the various satellites, and passes it on to similar larger stations round the world.

Two great motorways pass within six miles of Winkfield—the M3 at Bagshot and the M4 at Maidenhead; but the village is strenuously hanging on to its rural identity, and long may it survive.

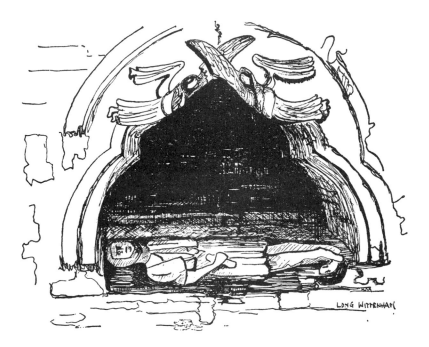

Long Wittenham

As its name implies, Long Wittenham sits all along a charming village street, midway between Wallingford and Abingdon. Behind it runs a backwater of the River Thames, and across the meadows Wittenham Clumps, the Sinodun Hills, rise up against the skyline.

Now a National Park, the Clumps are a favourite place for walkers and picnickers, and a fine new car park fills a long-felt want for sightseers; the B.F.W.I. recently planted a mature beech tree near the car-park, and long may it flourish.

Witta's Ham was the old Saxon name, and St. Birinus of Dorchester brought Christianity to the village in the 7th century. The present church of St. Mary was built of Caen stone about 1120, the third church on this site. It has an 850-years-old lead font, standing on its original base, and in the vestry is a recumbent effigy of a crusader only three feet long—said to be the smallest sculptured monument in England. The peal of six bells were recast in 1765 and the tenor bell is inscribed:

"Our voices shall with joyful sound
Make hills and valleys echo round".

Long Wittenham, with a population of 1,004 people, is one of the few villages that still keep up the May Queen ceremony; on May

1st, after the Queen is crowned, the children, carrying the traditional three-legged garlands, distribute posies to the older inhabitants.

Things to look for in Wittenham: The Pendon Museum with its model miniature village and railway museum, open only at weekends; St. Anthony's Well, whose waters traditionally have healing powers; the Saxon Village Cross; the Plough Inn, whose gardens go down to the River Thames; Willington's, a former Manor House; the remainder of the Village Cock Pit; the monks' stew ponds and a splendid old pigeon cote; all along the main road some fine old houses, including the 13th century Cruck Cottage.

The way called today The Maddy (Mead Way) leads to the parish boundary—the beautiful brick-built arched bridge designed by Sir George Gilbert Scott, where the traveller crosses over to Clifton Hampden and Oxfordshire.

Close by the bridge stands the Barley Mow Inn, the original structure being a "cruck" building dating from the 15th century. Here that timeless minor classic of the Thames was written—*Three Men in a Boat* by Jerome K. Jerome. Visitors to the Barley Mow can still be shown the Jerome Rooms.

Little Wittenham

Take the climbing and winding road across the fields to the west of Long Wittenham and you come to Little or West or Abbot's Wittenham. It sits under the Clumps and the road stops at the church—Little Wittenham's seventy inhabitants live in a gentle backwater.

St. Peter's Church, beautifully sited high above the Thames, has a mellow red-tiled roof, some of the finest memorial brasses in the country, and a delightful marble and alabaster monument to Walter Dunch, his nine children, and his wife, who was an aunt of Oliver Cromwell.

The steep path below the church crosses a bridge and comes to Day's Lock, one of the most attractive spots in Berkshire on a sunny day. Here you can watch the world "messing about in boats", picnic along the water meadows and on a hot day swim from one of the little sandy coves in the river bank.

Yateley means "gateway to a clearing in the forest". The area was part of the demesne of Heigh de Porte, taken from a Saxon lord and granted by William the Conqueror in recognition of services rendered.

The population at that time was about 30—now, after planned expansion, it is over 18,000.

All farms except one have been built over, but there are still many acres of common land and a village green with fishponds.

Instead of one elementary school that served the needs of the village not so long ago, there are now seven—ranging from infant to comprehensive—two private, and many nursery schools.

Yateley, with the remainder of the Rural District, is actually in Hampshire, though the postal address is Surrey; and to complicate things still further, the three Women's Institutes, Yateley, Yateley Green, and Yateley Venture belong to the Berkshire Federation!

The ancient church of St. Peter goes back, in part, to Norman and Saxon times. The son of a one-time Vicar of St. Peter's was Edward Caswall, translator of many hymns, and the congregation was no doubt often asked to "try out" these new hymns before Mr. Caswall made them public.

A mid-19th-century visiting preacher would assuredly have been Mr. Charles Kingsley, Rector of the adjoining parish of Eversley —poet, sportsman, expert angler, romanticist, and militant exponent of Protestantism and greatly loved author of *The Water Babies* and *Westward Ho!* A great walker and talker, Kingsley was often to be seen striding along the lanes, often with a fishing rod over his shoulder in case he found time for a quick cast over the Blackwater river; visiting someone sick perhaps, or giving a reading and writing lesson to some family; when he came as Rector to Eversley there were pitifully few adults who could write their own names.

This part of the country had a very unenviable reputation in the old days, and one who contributed in no small measure to this reputation of roughness was Parson Darby, another cleric who preached at Eversley and Yateley, but who supplemented his stipend by somewhat unorthodox means! He preached in the mornings and by night he was a highwayman, and most of the villagers around helped him in one way and another, and presumably got a "rake-off". In the end he was betrayed—by a village girl it is said, for he had a great eye for the ladies—and was duly hanged from a tree adjoining what is now known as Darby's Green.

Another notorious local lad was Charles Peace (not an apt name), later hanged for murdering a policeman.

169

Residents of whom Yateley can be more proud are Richard de Yateley, Abbot of Reading Abbey in 1405; Sir Stephen King-Hall, broadcaster and founder of the Hansard Society; Herman Darewski, song-writer and publisher; and Major Alan Murray, composer of *I'll walk beside you* and other songs.

It is said that, in 1605, Lord Mounteagle received, at Monteagle Farm, a letter warning him of the Gunpowder Plot. George III, wet and benighted, once spent a night sheltering in Yateley Mill—a mill which, with the church and its vicar, was described in *The House of Quiet* by A. G. Benson.

Just as those one-time "musts" of the nursery bookshelf—*Westward Ho!*, *Hereward the Wake*, and *Water Babies*—now tend to gather dust behind the paperbacks, so the description, by their author, Charles Kingsley, of the inhabitants of Yateley assuredly fits only a minute section of the 20,000 now living there:

". . . a thoroughly good fellow nevertheless. Civil, contented, industrious, and often very handsome; a far shrewder fellow, too—owing to his dash of wild forest blood, gipsy, highwayman and whatnot—than his bullet-headed and flaxen-polled cousin, the pure South Saxon of the chalk downs. . . ."

Yattendon

Here is a really beautiful village, compact, immaculately cared for, and set in lovely wooded country high in the downs. The centre of Yattendon is built round a wide road, almost a square, where a noble free-standing tree dominates the scene, and is aptly opposite the very attractive Royal Oak Inn.

The partly moated Manor House stands in a group of fine old buildings along the village street . . . the Manor, the Grange, the Church, the Rectory and the Malt House, all well worth looking for.

In the days of Henry VIII the Manor House belonged to the Norreys family, who entertained the King and his Queen—Katherine of Aragon, with her lady-in-waiting, Anne Boleyn. According to legend, the young Henry Norreys picked up a handkerchief for Anne, and this set in motion the sad events which led to her death and his execution as one of her lovers.

The church of St. Peter and St. Paul was built about 1450 on an earlier foundation. There is a fine Rood screen made by local carvers, and the enterprising members of a village class for copper-work made the copper font ewer and the brass candlesticks behind the south door.

A tragedy in 1956 led to the discovery of a number of deep and forgotten wells in old houses around Yattendon. Mrs. Faithfull, in the Royal Oak Inn, fell to her death 134 feet in a well that suddenly opened in the floor. Many tons of flint were used to seal up the opening, and other wells were made safe.

Frilsham, an extension of Yattendon with some old cottages and much new housing, has now been separated from Yattendon by the M4 Motorway which cuts right through superb unspoiled country and beechwoods. The little church of St. Frideswide, originally Saxon with Norman and later additions, has an almost unique round churchyard, which indicates a pagan origin.

Frilsham Manor, which also belonged to the Norreys family, and Frilsham House, are the two large dwellings in this small village. A daughter of the Berties of Frilsham House created a local gossip by marrying one Gallini, dancing-master to George I.

On a beautiful site among the beechwoods is the Frilsham Village Hall and sports ground, with superb views over some of the loveliest unspoilt countryside in Berkshire.

Between the villages of Yattendon and Frilsham are some curious and interesting chalk caves. In a meadow where wild daffodils grow is the site of an old house destroyed in the Civil Wars, when its owners fled for their lives leaving all their gold and treasures in a well for safety.

Although many attempts have been made, the buried treasure has never been recovered, and local legend says that the long dead owner haunts the meadow.

Take your camera with you when you visit Yattendon and Frilsham . . . there is much to delight the discerning eye.

Interesting People

Henry Addington, Lord Sidmouth, lived at Earley and was educated at Reading School.

Alfred the Great, born at Wantage, won the battle of Ashdown against the Danes on the Berkshire Downs.

Simon Alwyn, who changed his religion 3 times, was the immortal Vicar of Bray.

George Arliss, actor, lived at Pangbourne.

Lena Ashwell, Lady Simpson, the actress, lived at Chieveley until her death.

Herbert Asquith, Lord. Oxford and Asquith, Prime Minister, lived at Sutton Courtenay.

Roger Bacon, had an observatory at Sunninghill.

William Backhouse, who lived at Swallowfield, invented a pedometer in 1628.

Sir Benjamin Baker, builder of the Forth Bridge, lived at Pangbourne.

Thomas Barham, who wrote "The Ingoldsby Legend", stayed at Uffington with the Hughes family.

Hannibal Baskerville, lived at Sunningwell. His father was a General, he had 32 Captains as godfathers, and 18 children.

H. M. Bateman, cartoonist, lived at Curridge.

St. Thomas à Becket, consecrated Reading Abbey in 1168.

Thomas Bekynton, secretary of King Henry VI was Rector of Sutton Courtenay and often stayed at The Abbey.

Archbishop Benson, was the first Headmaster at Wellington College.

Lawrence Binyon, poet, is buried at Aldworth.

St. Birinus preached at Long Wittenham and at Churn Nob near Blewbury.

R. D. Blackmore, author of "Lorna Doone" was born at Longworth.

Sir William Blackstone, eminent lawyer, lived at Wallingford.

Lord Bolingbroke, Tory statesman, lived at Bucklebury.

Elizabeth, 2nd wife of King Robert Bruce, was imprisoned at Bisham.

Bishop Butler, born at Wantage, son of a Presbyterian draper, wrote "The Analogy of Religion".

Mr. Bunce, of Ashbury, invented a snow-plough.

Edmund Campion, Roman Catholic martyr and saint, was captured at Lyford on Ock, and executed afterwards.

George Canning, Prime Minister, stayed at Easthampstead.

King Canute, according to legend, had a palace at Cherbury near Charney Bassett.

Lewis Carroll, author of "Alice in Wonderland" visited Cranbourne Vicarage.

Mrs. Neville Chamberlain, wife of the Prime Minister, lived at West Woodhay.

Thomas Chaucer, son of the poet, lived at Buckland House in the 15th Century.

Cherry-Garrard, Antarctic explorer, lived at Denford House, Hungerford.

Sir John Conroy, doctor to the Duchess of Kent, mother of Queen Victoria, lived at Arborfield.

Miles Coverdale, first translator of the whole Bible into English, lived at Newbury in 1539.

William, Duke of Cumberland, victor of Culloden, bred the famous race-horse, Eclipse, at Windsor.

David Davies, Rector of Barkham, wrote the 18th century standard work on agricultural wages.

Thomas Day, author of "Sandford and Merton", was killed in a riding accident and is buried at Wargrave.

Lord Desborough, the famous oar, was High Steward of Bray.

Claude Duval, highwayman, had a house at Bagshot.

Edward, the Black Prince, owned Prince's Manor, Harwell.

John Elwes, miser and M.P. lived at Marcham.

John Fell, Bishop of Oxford, subject of the famous rhyme "I do not love thee, Dr. Fell", was born at Longworth and lived at Sunningwell where he is buried.

Elijah Fenton, poet, is buried at Easthampstead.

Sir Luke Fildes, painted "The Village Wedding" at Blewbury.

Alice FitzWaryn, wife of Dick Whittington, lived at Wantage.

Arabella Fermor, of Ufton Nervet, was the original Belinda, heroine of "The Rape of the Lock" by Alexander Pope.

Dick Francis, champion rider and author of racing novels, lives at Blewbury.

Piers Gaveston, favourite of Edward II, owned the Manor of Harwell.

Dr. Geoffrey Goodman, entertained King Charles I at West Ilsley.

Lady Catherine Gordon, lived at Fyfield. One of her 4 husbands was Perkin Warbeck, the impostor.

W. G. Grace, used to play bowls at Hurley.

Earl Haig, lived at Cranbourne.

Sir Edward Hannes, doctor to Queen Anne, lived at Shillingford.

David Hartley, signatory to the Peace Treaty between Great Britain and the U.S.A. in 1783, owned East Shefford.

Warren Hastings, lived at Purley Hall from 1788 to 1794, and is reputed to haunt the house.

Jerome K. Jerome wrote "Three Men in a Boat" at The Barley Mow in Long Wittenham.

Sir William Jones, Attorney General to Charles II, owned Weston in 1679. He is remembered as "bull-faced Jonas" in Dryden's "Absolom and Ahitophel".

Speaker William Lenthall, the regicide, lived at Besselsleigh.

Thomas Lamplugh, Archbishop of York, was Rector of Binfield.

Archbishop Laud, born in Reading, a pupil at Reading School, secured the Royal Charter for his birthplace.

Richard Lovelace, romantic poet, lived at Hurley, and was Lord Lieutenant of Berkshire.

John Lovelace, son of Richard, plotted the downfall of James II at Ladye Place, Hurley.

Sir John Mason, who "outwitted the Italian, and out-graved the Don in Spain", was born in Abingdon.

Marc Antonio de Dominus, Archbishop of Spalato, Dean of Windsor, and Rector of West Ilsley, was the first person to explain the phenomenon of the rainbow.

Miss Mary Mitford, who wrote "Our Village", is buried at Swallowfield.

Mrs. Montague, the original "blue stocking", lived at Sandleford Priory.

Sir Thomas More, Chancellor to Henry VIII, Roman Catholic Saint and Martyr. His descendants still live at East Hendred.

Owen Nares, popular actor, lived at Sonning.

John Newbury, the first publisher of books for children, was born at Waltham St. Lawrence.

Henry Norreys, who lived at the Manor House, Yattendon, was beheaded as one of the lovers of Anne Boleyn.

Ivor Novello, actor and composer, wrote "Perchance to Dream", while living at Red Roofs, Littlewick Green.

George Orwell, author of "Animal Farm", is buried at Sutton Courtenay.

William Penn, founder of Pennsylvania, U.S.A., was born and lived at Ruscombe. He was a Quaker who went to America in 1668 to escape from religious persecution.

Peter the Great, Tsar of Russia, visited Milton House to see Admiral Benbow.

Matthew Prior, who lived at Little Wittenham, wrote "Henry and Emma", described by Austin Dobson as "an almost unendurable didactic work".

Edward Pococke, Arabic scholar, lived at the Old Rectory, Childrey, in 1646.

Alexander Pope, poet, lived at Binfield as a young man.

Stephen Poyntz, tutor of the Duke of Cumberland, lived at Midgham.

Miss Baden-Powell founded the Girl Guide movement at Pinkneys Green in 1910.

Henry Powle, Speaker of William III's first parliament, lived at Shottesbrooke.

Henry Pye, poet-laureate, was born at Faringdon. His constant allusions to "feathered choirs" and "vocal groves" provoked the saying "When the PYE was open the birds began to sing".

Rainbald, Chancellor to Edward the Confessor and Abbot of Cirencester, founded the Church of St. Andrew's, East Hagbourne.

Field-Marshal Lord Roberts lived at Ascot.

Sir W. Gilbert Scott, architect, designed the packhorse bridge at Clifton Hampden.

Emily Sellwood, wife of Alfred, Lord Tennyson, lived at Pibworth House, Aldworth, before her marriage.

John Stair, produced the William Pear at Aldermaston.

Alice, Duchess of Suffolk, changed sides in the Wars of the Roses, and became Custodian of Wallingford Castle.

Dean Swift, author of "Gulliver's Travels" was a frequent visitor to the Rectory at Letcombe Bassett.

Sir Herbert Beerbohm Tree frequently stayed at Binfield Rectory.

John Walter, founder of *The Times* newspaper, lived at Bearwood, Wokingham.

Wilhelmina, Queen of the Netherlands, lived at Stubbings House, Burchetts Green, as an exile from the Nazi occupation of Holland.

William of Wykeham, owned Lollington in Cholsey, in 1392. He began his career at Windsor Castle as keeper of the King's dogs, at the wage of 3 farthings a day.

Lord Zetland, Secretary of State for India in 1939, lived at Snelsmore.

Notable Monumental Brasses

Appleton John Goodryngton, in shroud, 1518.
Ashbury John de Walden, Thomas de Bussbury, William Skelton.
Basildon John Clerk and wife.
Binfield Walter de Anneford, 1361.
Blewbury John Balam, priest, 1496. Sir John Daunce and wife, 1523, 1548.
Bray John de Foxley, John Rixman and others.
Brightwell John Scoffyld, Priest with chalice, and others.
Buckland John Yates and wife, 1578, and 12 children.
Burghfield Nicholas Williams and wife, 1568.
Childrey a large collection of brasses dated from 1444 to 1529.
Cholsey John Mere, priest with chalice, 1471.
Compton Richard Pygott and wife, 1520.
Cookham Babham family, and others.
Coxwell (Great) William Morys, 1509. Lady, 1510.
Cumnor Anthony Forster and others.
Denchworth Hyde family.
East Hendred Henry Eldersley, 1439. John Eyston, 1589.
Finchampstead Elizabeth Blighe and daughter 1635.
Harwell John Jennens and wife, 1599.
Hatford Francis Pigott, 1614.
Hurst Richard Ward and wife, 1574. A lady in bed, 1600.
Kintbury John Gunter and wife, 1626.
Lambourn Eastbury family and others, 1406 to 1619.
Letcombe Regis A lady, 1440.
Longworth Priest and others.
Remenham Knight, 1591. Priest, 1622.
Marcham Edward Fettiplace and family.
Old Windsor Mitchell family portraits.
Sandhurst Richard Geale and wife, 1608.
Shefford (Little) John Fetyplace, 1524.
Shottesbrooke Priest and Civilian, 1370, and others.
Sonning Lawrence Fyton, 1434, and others.
Sparsholt Priest in Cross, 1353. John Fettiplace and others.
Stanford-Dingley Margaret Dyneley, 1444, and others.
Stanford-in-the-Vale Roger Campedene, 1398.
Steventon Richard Do and wife, Edmund Wiseman and family.
Stratfield-Mortimer Richard Trevet, 1441 and lady.
Streatley Thomas Buriton and family.
Swallowfield Christopher Lytkott and wife, 1554.
Tidmarsh Margaret Wode, 1499.
Upton Nervet William Smith and wife, 1627.
White Waltham Lady, 1445.
Wantage Collection of five, 1360 to 1619.
Welford 2 small priests.
Windsor Various.
Winkfield A yeoman of the guard, 1630.
Wittenham (Little) Various, 1433 to 1683.
Yattendon Algernon Simeon, 1924.

175

INDEX